Cultu...
the Ca...

...nce, cruelty, ...Carnival of ...at an over-...l desire for ...al pleasure. This ...ire h... suited in a cat... ...it pleasures often ...med criminal by those in pow...

...mongst the fascinating issues Mike Presdee addresses are:

- the ... ing out of carnival desires on the streets through joy-riding, street crime and antisocial behaviour, and in private via the Internet;
- the commodification of hate, hurt and humiliation in popular culture;
- the popularisation and criminalisation of sadomasochism and dance music cultures.

The author concludes that in order to truly make sense of senseless acts, it is essential for criminologists to turn to cultural criminology and that, as successive governments take steps to further rationalise public life, they will continue to create crime rather than to alleviate it.

Mike Presdee is currently Reader in the Department of Sociology and Social Policy at Sunderland University, and Visiting Senior Research Fellow in the Sociology Department at the University of Kent. In the past he has variously served as a Royal Marines commando, lived on the streets in Canada and advised government ministers on matters concerning young people and crime.

Cultural Criminology and the Carnival of Crime

Mike Presdee

London and New York

First published 2000
by Routledge
11 New Fetter Lane, London EC4P 4EE

Simultaneously published in the USA and Canada
by Routledge
29 West 35th Street, New York, NY 10001

Reprinted 2001

Routledge is an imprint of the Taylor & Francis Group

© 2000 Mike Presdee

Typeset in Sabon by RefineCatch Limited, Bungay, Suffolk
Printed and bound in Great Britain by
TJ International Ltd, Padstow, Cornwall

British Library Cataloguing in Publication Data
A catalogue record for this book is available from the British Library

Library of Congress Cataloging in Publication Data
Presdee, Mike
    Cultural criminology and the carnival of crime / Mike Presdee
        p. cm.
    Includes bibliographical references and index.
    1. Crime – Sociological aspects.   2. Criminology.   3. Deviant
behavior.   4. Subculture.   5. Pleasure – Social aspects.   I. Title.
HV6150.P74   2000
364 – dc21   00–032824

ISBN 0–415–23909–5 (hbk)
ISBN 0–415–23910–9 (pbk)

Contents

To GG
Ceinwen, Merren, Hannah
and Chloe

Apologies

I have spent most of my life apologising for all that I have done or not done. When I am bumped into in a shop or the street I usually end up apologising for getting in the way of some superior being. A sort of apology for daring to exist. A part of the residual culture of working-class deference that is still part of my social make-up. I have no intention of disguising this pathetic trait now and as such I have some apologies to make.

To Steven Gerrard, Caroline Wintersgill and Mari Shullaw for taking so much time that Steven and Caroline moved on in their publishing careers leaving Mari to suffer alone. To Sandra Jones for introducing her to the dark world of dead rappers. To Gavin Carver for emptying his cellar and his head for the last three years. To all those whom I hope read what I have written for not being clear enough or exciting enough. To my colleagues in Criminology and Cultural Studies for failing to get over what we all want to say. I hand over the baton to them. To Reece (Rear Gunner) Walters for not mastering the time difference between the United Kingdom and New Zealand and ringing too often and too late. To Pam Abbott for not ringing enough. To John Muncie for unsettling and upsetting both his diet and his fridge. To Chris Hale for not calling him enough. To Maggie O'Neill for not dancing around her handbag enough. To Ian Taylor, Kit Carsons, Ken Good, John O'Neill and Terry O'Connor-Mason, for not listening carefully enough. To Paul Willis for failing the Real

Ale test. To Jan McKemmish and Helen Barnes for never arriving when I said I would. To Claire Wallace for never arriving and to Kris O'Connor-Mason for arriving too often. To Olwen and John Harrison for practising ideas on them too much. To Alison Packer, Jo Lee, James Copland, Tim Ellis, Hugh Girling and Sarah Frost for being grumpy for three years. To Jeff Ferrell, Mark Hamm and Ken Tunnell for enjoying their music and their mind bending too much. To all those whom I have slept with for snoring too much. To all my friends for enjoying life too much and to my employers for seemingly not enjoying work enough. To my bank manager for not being solvent for the entire period it took to write this book and to my doctor for carelessly losing six pints of blood towards the end of it. To Carol for having hair too long, for too long. To my family for not being there enough and to Gill for not loving enough and lastly to my father for wanting too much.

Acknowledgements

The author and publishers would like to thank the following for granting permission to reproduce material in this work:

Condé Nast Publications for allowing us to reproduce the cover of the March 1999 issue of *GQ* magazine.

Duckworth Finn Grubb Waters advertising agency for allowing us to reproduce their 1999 Virgin Radio advertisement.

The Iron Bed Company and Saatchi & Saatchi for allowing us to reproduce their 1999/2000 advertisements.

Metal Morphosis for allowing us to reproduce their piercing menu.

A. P. Watt Ltd on behalf of Michael B. Yeats for allowing us to reproduce lines from 'Among Social Children' by W. B. Yeats.

Every effort has been made to contact copyright holders for their permission to reprint material in this book. The publishers would be grateful to hear from any copyright holder who is not here acknowledged and will undertake to rectify any errors or omissions in future editions of this book.

1 Introduction

In the last two weeks of April 1999 there were a number of horrendous international and national events, the accumulation of which brought into sharp focus the nature of life in contemporary industrial societies. In a school in Denver, Colorado there was the 'Trench coat' massacre, followed the next week by a similar shoot-out in Alberta, Canada. The very next week five young men in New York were arrested for plotting a similar fate for their school and fellow students. This was followed by the death of 45 people in tornados. In Britain there were three nail bomb attacks in the London areas of Brixton, Brick Lane and Soho, the last of which was placed in a crowded gay bar with devastating results. This followed seven days of armed sieges both in London and the north-west of England and, in London, the well-known British television presenter Jill Dando was executed on her own doorstep, creating media mass-mourning throughout the country. In the Netherlands Dutch police shot four soccer 'hooligans' whilst Moroccan soccer fans went on the rampage throughout the rest of the country. All of this happened in the middle of the Kosovan War, where the images and sounds of daily death and destruction became the standard fare of most of the media of the Western world, interspersed with the 'gripping' and 'entertaining' footage of people being destroyed by either human or natural disasters. The school siege in Denver was relayed to the world 'live' as television cameras followed the drama with a running commentary being given by trapped students on their mobile phones. Tornado destruction was followed eagerly by both professional cameras and the amateur camcorder.

Politicians, pundits and the media had a field day with predictions of the end of civilisation as we know it. The cartoon in the 2 May's *Sunday Times* depicted the word 'CIVILISATION' blown to pieces and splattered with blood, whilst the Prime Minister felt the need to write his own column in the *Sunday Times* where he stated, 'The bombers will fail because they are not part of modern Britain. They are the real outsiders in society. The minority.' He went on to call the culprits 'evil thugs' and then used the rest of his statement to defend his and Nato's bomb violence in the Balkans, thereby giving the message that it wasn't the violence that was wrong but it was more a question of who used it and for what reason. Indeed, the Prime Minister through his actions confirmed to both the national and international communities that: 'Violence may change the direction of violence, invert the roles of violation and victim, but it necessarily affirms the principle of violence whatever else it achieves' (Kappeler 1995: 258). It was as if the ability to control violence on a personal level and control violence at the level of the state were unconnected. Yet the Labour government's then Secretary of State for Northern Ireland, Dr Mo Mowlam, reiterated in a statement on 26 August 1999 that she was 'in no doubt that all violence, for whatever reason it is perpetuated, is unacceptable'.

However, the general targets for blame quickly became 'young people', as always, along with the notion of 'evil', as well as a whole collection of the usual scapegoats such as television and the Internet, as the whole of the 'chattering classes' tried to fathom out what was going on in Western civilisation. Almost all the newspapers carried articles from the Internet on how to buy weapons and how to make bombs, with page after page on how to conduct a successful war in the Balkans. The speculation as to who murdered Jill Dando and why was coupled with daily articles on how you would go about hiring a hit-man if you wanted to, how much it would cost and how a hit-man might go about it. The *Observer* carried the story ' "Two in the head, one in the heart": Tony Thompson is told how an expert hitman would have done it.' (2/5/99). The *Observer* newspaper obviously realised that this was a service they could provide their readers, as if we all had someone we wanted dead and that this sort of service was commonplace. The *Sunday Times* carried the headline 'Children of 14 carry guns for "status" ' with a photograph of ten-year-old Americans brandishing automatic weapons and the warning that 'now they are spreading to Britain' (*Sunday Times* 9/5/99). Yet at the same time there was throughout Britain a general feeling of fascination tinged with fear for a world that appeared to be rapidly turning 'upside down'. Crime and violence seemed to have saturated all of life to the extent that for a while there seemed nothing else.

This book is an attempt to enter the murky waters of explanation. It is an attempt to put some pieces of the puzzle of crime, violence and transgression together to help us make sense of what goes on around us. Labelling all acts that we don't understand as 'evil' leads us nowhere. It is in the end an intellectual cop-out that leads us away from the analysis of society and culture and guides us instead into the realm of the spiritual and the unknown and the unfathomable forces of darkness where we can have little or no effect and where we have no responsibility to understand. It persuades us that we have no need to look at our society, only that we need to examine inside the mind of the 'evil' individual.

I believe, however, that the context in which crime and violence are acted out is of paramount importance, and that an analytical 'cultural criminology' is necessary to achieve any in-depth understanding of crime, including violent crime and so-called 'senseless' acts.

As Norbert Elias eloquently pointed out in the early 1980s,

> As things are, one may even fail to recognise violent action between or within states as a human-made catastrophe. Social scientists have not yet succeeded in

demonstrating convincingly that killing is no answer to killing, whether in a good or bad cause. Nor have they succeeded in making it more widely known and also better understood that cycles of violence, whether they are kept in motion by integration or by hegemonial struggles, by class conflicts or by interstate conflicts, have strong self-escalating tendencies. War processes, for example, are difficult to stop even if they are still in the preparatory state of reciprocal threats of violence creeping towards its use. They almost invariably breed professional killers of one kind or another, whether these killers have the social character of dictator or general, of freedom fighter or mercenary. Their impulses and their actions are geared to mutual suspicion, hatred and violence: as levers of human catastrophes they are to be feared no less than the plague which once seemed to humans equally uncontrollable.

(Quoted in Goudsblom and Mennell 1998: 86)

The fascination with violence and crime clearly experienced in the final two weeks of April 1999 described above shows that there is also potential entertainment value to be realised from such acts. These 'stories' point clearly to the 'violence of human possibility and imagination' that Schechner (1988) talks about. The way that we enjoy violence, crime, humiliation and hurt is part of the equation and needs to be examined and thought through. Even the enjoyment of doing wrong, which many of us have felt at some time in our lives, becomes important as it puts us all in some sense 'in touch' with crime, connecting us to it in an emotional way so that we become acquainted with the emotions of criminal life through our own transgressions. Indeed, crime is as much about emotions – hatred, anger, frustration, excitement and love – as it is about poverty, possessing and wealth. In a society such as ours where emotion stands against the rational and material world, those without wealth are left only with the world of emotions to express their hurts, their injustices and their identity. Their transgressions, arising as they do from this world of emotions, are as a consequence seeped in emotive elements.

Rage, anger and hatred are commonplace characteristics in the performance of crime.

The feeling of 'getting away with it' that comes as part of doing wrong, the buzz and excitement of the act of doing wrong itself, of living on the 'edge' of law and order, are all emotions that many seek out in the daily performance of their lives. Indeed, in a society where 'compassion fatigue' (Mestrovic 1997) is common, the seeking out of increasingly heightened emotional experiences becomes more and more a part of everyday life. The author Anthony Burgess in his autobiography, *You've Had Your Time*, explained his own self-disgust at his emotions when creating the violence of his novel *A Clockwork Orange* (1996) when he commented, 'I was sickened by my own excitement at setting it down'. Here he recognised how his emotions had transgressed the rules of rationality and that there was something in his cultural inheritance that had led him to revel in and be excited by violence. Indeed, he requested that the film version of his novel, which concentrated on the violence, be withheld from the British viewing public.

Enjoyment, desire and pleasure are then important features of social life and in some way they are both transposed into cultural forms and emanate from them. Richard Schechner (1988) again points out that representations found and experienced as cultural artefacts are 'evidence of the violence of desire, its twisted and dangerous possibilities'. Desire becomes the engine that drives us to seek out certain cultural acts whilst the resulting pleasure drives desire once again to find new limits. Gilles Deleuze points to the 'sensualness' of 'wickedness' when he identified two kinds of wrong-doing, the one 'unthought out and common' and the other 'self-conscious and sensualised and intelligent' (1997: 37). And Elias talked of how human groups took a 'strange delight in asserting their superiority over others, particularly if it has been attained by violent means' (Goudsblom and Mennell 1998: 89).

In the case of the Colorado killings, much was made of the young killer's 'Goth' culture and fascination with Goth music and its focus on death, dying and darkness. (This reported interest in Goth culture was something that was later shown to be untrue.) This crude attempt to connect youth sub-cultures with murder continued in the week following the Soho bombings, when the *Observer* newspaper similarly reported a neighbour of the three arrested men as saying,

> They would wear black baggy clothes and T-shirts with 'Iron Maiden' written on them. Their friends used to come round and they all seemed to be in Gothic clothes, looking like they were in a band.
>
> (*Observer* 2/5/99)

In the *Sunday Times* the same witness talked of a man whom he 'thought looked like a computer nerd. Both the men used to wear mainly black clothes and I saw them wearing Iron Maiden T-shirts'. Andrew Marr writing in the *Observer* noted:

> There has been a lot of nonsense talked about the spe-cially evil influence of the shock-rock star Marilyn Man-son, adored by the Denver boy killers. He looks like a rather amateur copy of Alice Cooper . . . poseur-Satanists have infected popular music for decades. But there are under-cultures on the net, Gothic necro-fantasy which can grip kids going through that gloomy phase when one's body is erupting with chemicals.
>
> (*Observer* 2/5/99)

Whilst others talked of 'psychopathy as a fashion accessory' (*Guardian* 8/5/99), the film actor Leonardo DiCaprio declared he would never again appear in a violent movie.

No matter what we feel about these statements, it is clear that cultural forms and artefacts are an important element in our everyday lives and as such we quickly come into conflict, through the seeking of pleasure, with the dominant perspec-tives on life. It is here that we enter the realm of challenge, control, resistance and even carnival. It is here somewhere in the process of culture formation and identity formation that the criminalisation process itself begins. The response by authority to the unfathomable is to outlaw and to criminalise; this is part of the process of the criminalisation of what Chris Rojek calls the 'deviant leisure' of the oppressed and the dispossessed (Rojek 1995: 99).

What follows in this book is, in part, about pleasure, the performance of pleasure, the display of pleasure and the consumption of pleasure. (Part I attempts to analyse and Part II to contextualise.) Such pleasures are not of course universal; in a desire to exercise their pleasures, a certain group will inevitably displease others – at times directly, at other times indirectly. In some cases the construction of displeasure for some is the very fount of pleasure for others. As Deleuze points out, 'The strange relationship between pleasure in doing and pleasure in suffering evil has always been sensed by doctors and writers who have recorded man's intimate life' (Deleuze 1997: 38). Christopher Lasch too recognises the relationship between pleasure, desire and commodity production:

> In a society that has reduced reason to mere calculation, reason can impose no limits on the pursuit of pleasure – on the immediate gratification of every desire no matter how perverse, insane, criminal, or merely immoral. For the standards that would condemn crime or cruelty derive from religion, compassion, or the kind of reason that rejects purely instrumental applications and none of these outmoded forms of thought or feeling has any logical place in a society based on commodity production.
>
> (Lasch 1979: 69)

Excitement, even ecstasy (the abandonment of reason and rationale), is the goal of the performance of many of the dramas related here. The quest for excitement is directly related to the breaking of boundaries, of confronting parameters and playing at the margins of social life in the challenging of controllers and their control mechanisms.

Further I am concerned here, in the main, with pleasure sought and gained on the margins of social life and, more to the point, the illegal performance of those pleasures.

Much of this book is concerned with that part of life described by Bakhtin as the 'second life of the people' (Bakhtin 1984). It is from the second life of the people that the majority of 'transgressions' emanate. It is here that we find the genesis and rationale for behaviour that anticipates the ability to destroy, disrupt and dissent. The second life of the people is that part of life that is inaccessible and untouchable to the 'official' world of the scientific rationality of modernity and its politics, parties and politicians. It is the realm of resentment and irrationality *par excellence* and also the realm of much crime. It is that part of social life that is unknowable to those in power and which therefore stands outside their consciousness and their understanding. They cannot understand it or indeed even 'read' it as real life, but only as immoral, uncivilised, obscene and unfathomable social behaviour.

However, as politicians attempt to bend social life through social policies so it leaves us all without a 'usable past' to give direction to our lives, forcing us into the realm of the second life (Holquist 1984). In the end there becomes no differentiation between carnival and true life, the second life, where the only laws are the laws of freedom with no possibility of any real life outside of it. This unofficial life is where we express our fears of rational official life, with its meanings and consequences, its poverty and accompanying pains of inequality. This second life is where everyday life resides and where the rationality of law loses its power.

This second festive life expressed through carnival acts cannot be expressed in official rational life where it quickly becomes criminalised and demonised. It is a life that is expressed through the world of excess, obscenity and degradation. It becomes the only true site for the expression of one's true feelings for life. It is where the irrational laughs and mocks the rational – where truth can be told against the cold-hearted lies of rational, scientific modernity. The second life is lived in the cracks and holes in the structures of official society. It searches for and finds the unpunishable whilst official society seeks to dam up the holes and fill in the cracks, criminalising as it does and making punishable the previously unpunishable. The second life is characterised by 'freedom, equality and abundance' (Bakhtin 1984: 9), whilst official life is lived in a world of oppression, inequality and poverty where carnival seeks to assert itself every day and through the everyday, making the second life the only real life with any real meaning. The expression of the second life of the people is performed and brought to life through carnival, which becomes for rational society understood as no more or less than the carnival of crime.

The process of violence involved is about powerlessness and meaninglessness and the loosening of cultural imperatives. In short it is about the total estrangement from the powerful. It is that part of life that celebrates the irrational, celebrates the incomprehensible, celebrates the crude, celebrates the nothingness of being powerless. This celebration of disrespect is manifested through the theatre of carnival, the debris of which is to be found in the daily performances and acting out of ordinary everyday lives. The world of the rational fragments the world of the irrational so that the 'second life of the people', no longer controlled and contained by traditional carnival, disintegrates and breaks away. The resulting debris of carnival now resides and takes refuge in the 'everyday' lived life of the 'other' world. It is a world characterised by defiance and the destruction of meaning. It is an untouchable world based on the threat of the bizarre, beyond the reach of the rational. It is a world where the 'fart' rather than the 'thought' is of more importance. It is truly the world of the carnival of crime.

> The rules that come with the process of 'acquiring' and 'ownership' seemed more difficult to accept than those of stealing time and place. Stealing time, although an offence, was easier to hide and explain, but stealing 'possessions' was more complex, for whereas stealing 'time'

could get you the sack, stealing 'possessions' could get you gaol. But why was it that some people were allowed possessions and others not? Why did some have bikes and others not? Some big homes and others not? Some honey and others not? Increasingly, as I got older, I became more sensitive about displaying myself and my everyday possessions that enabled people at a glance to 'place me'; know where I was from and so know when I was 'straying'; when I was out of my place. The accoutrements of class were becoming like a uniform, displaying my rank and position to everyone. I began to feel ashamed of my sewn-up satchel from 'Woolies', that stood out from the shiny leather ones hanging on the backs of other desks; and I sulked quietly in the corner of the changing rooms trying not to bring attention to my old-fashioned brown football boots, which appeared museum pieces compared to the black, shiny, low-cut modern boots pulled on by others.

From my shame slowly developed both defiance and aggression as I excessively and openly consumed all that I stole, displaying my fragile and dishonest wealth to everyone; a rather dishevelled and unkempt young boy growing fat and angry. As I put on weight, so I learned to push it around; and when I was ridiculed because of my hefty and ugly black metal-studded school boots, I responded in playground soccer games in a manner that got me a reputation of a cruel, efficient full-back who would knock you down or break your legs. Those fancy, well-cut, Bata shoes had no deterrent effect compared with a fully studded black boot aimed at defenceless shins. I started to learn about violence as an answer to ridicule, and I started to glorify ugliness, learning how to disrupt the sensitivities of those from more sophisticated backgrounds. I learned who would be offended by a fart or a belch, by leaning on the wall, by a tie hanging down, by a cap not straight: I would show them what I thought of their sophistication, their manners, their world!

(Presdee 1988)

I have moved a long way from talk about death, destruction and 'senseless acts' to the criminalisation of culture and everyday life, but it is my contention that the two are intimately linked and are part and parcel of the same debate. It is a difficult debate because it challenges what authority thinks is 'right' and makes connections between our 'right' lives and others' 'wrong' lives. It puts us in the same box as those we consider criminal and as such makes the very thought uncomfortable and unthinkable. To suggest that there is any connection between those who perpetrate violence and ourselves is of course unthinkable but it may be true. To suggest that those who gain satisfaction through S&M relationships should be legally allowed to do so is unthinkable yet may be the right way to go. To think that crime might in some way be enjoyable to us all is difficult to grapple with and unpleasant to think about. I am not advocating that violence is right, that crime is right, that pleasure at all costs is right, only that we need to think through honestly the connection between culture and crime. We need to countenance the fact that crime and violence erupt out of social processes and come from within social life not from outside of it. By regarding the extremes as outside of our society we put them outside of our consciousness and outside of our thinking. Out of sight, out of mind. We need to be able to make sense of marginalised groups not make them invisible. We need a criminology that knows they're there and has the ability to 'read' them, indeed we need to know and want to know why they are marginalised and criminalised in the first place and how the process works. We need a criminology that understands that crime itself has become a valuable consumer entertainment commodity, to be enjoyed and consumed daily through modern media and communication processes. We need a criminology that grapples with the question as to where acts of hurt, harm and hate come from and how such actions have permeated contemporary culture in such a 'fun' way that we are no longer ashamed of our lust for violence. We need a criminology that can comment on how culture kills. That death by dancing or death by media can and does happen.

We need to make sense of rather than sensationalise all of this.

I hope that this book makes some contribution to this debate. That it at least closes doors if not opens them; asks questions if not answers them; motivates others to ask similar questions and creates debate. It is an argument for the necessity for both a cultural criminology and a passionate criminology, that can truly attempt to understand the richness of responses to the economic structures that surround us, that we all act out during what we have come simply to call 'life'.

> I did wrong right from the beginning. There at the start, when rules are first brought to bear on us, and we start to learn about control; who the controllers are and what's being controlled. The first lesson was in how to control ourselves; how to control our bodily functions; how to use a potty and when; bringing together both a sense of time and place – just after meals – last thing at night – once a day. 'A time and a place for everything.' This early form of self-oppression was something I never really conquered until I was ten and only then after years of soiled beds and bed clothes, which increased the already heavy load of washing, drying and ironing that faced my mother.
>
> (Presdee 1988)

Part I
Analysis

2 Cultural criminology

Above all else this book is concerned with the criminalisation of everyday life and the meanings of crime. It is about the way that our everyday responses to a modern, highly commodified consumer society become themselves defined as criminal. In this chapter I examine the interrelationships between culture, crime and a specific form of criminology, namely cultural criminology, that attempts to unravel and make sense of the processes whereby cultural forms and cultural expressions themselves become criminalised (Ferrell and Sanders 1995). Indeed all that follows uses the methodologies of the cultural criminologist in an attempt to understand more fully, in all its complexity, the interrelationship between culture and crime. Cultural criminology uses the 'evidence' of everyday existence, wherever it is found and in whatever form it can be found; the debris of everyday life is its 'data'. It uses cultural artefacts whenever and wherever they present themselves, examining the cultural 'trail' they leave behind. Life histories, images, music and dance, all have a story to tell in the unravelling of crime. Such stories tell us more about the nature of crime than a report full of statistics as the 'traces of the storyteller cling to the story the way hand prints of the potter cling to the clay vessel' (Benjamin 1970: 91). Our lives and those of others are rich in experience, in turn transposed into cultural forms to be carefully and honestly dissected. Here the 'qualitative' becomes the flesh on the bones of 'quantitative' criminology and its 'brief' is both kaleidoscopic and multifaceted, exploring and attempting to make sense of the senseless, the forbidden and the outlawed. It pushes the perspectives of conventional criminology beyond its horizon. Yet '[b]ending or breaking the boundaries of criminology to construct a cultural criminology in this sense does not undermine contemporary criminology as much as it expands and enlivens it' (Ferrell and Sanders 1995: 17).

Like all those interested in crime and the effects of crime on the victim, the criminal and society, cultural criminology is interested in the larger movements at work in contemporary society. That is, the social context in which crime comes into being and is played out: in short, the criminalising process. What is important for cultural criminology is to examine 'everything that happens before crime occurs', as 'the question of what precedes crime is far more critical to our understanding than the act of crime itself' (Quinney 1994: 1).

We need continually to remind ourselves of one single simple statement, that a criminal act has to be defined through social and cultural processes that are in themselves played out separate from the essence of the act itself. For example, the act of taking a life does not become 'murder' until defined as such through the discourses of the powerful. It is these cultural discourses that both designate and define any particular act as criminal. Until the context has been designated and defined by the powerful as a criminal one, the act of taking a life may be defined as right, desirable, even good, as well as, unthinkably, pleasurable. As Joanna Bourke argues, acts that are criminalised in civilian life are discovered by men in wartime to be pleasurable as they 'discover the pleasures of killing' and a 'macabre delight in the act of destroying other human lives which border at times on the erotic' (Bourke 1999: 15). To kill in the Balkans was defined by Tony Blair as the 'right' thing to do, no matter how 'regrettable', no matter if we kill the wrong person. In this context the act of killing becomes defined by those in power as 'right'. The political processes of the powerful have the ability to make criminals of us one day and heroes the next. It is this criminalising process that provides the fertile ground for the eruption of carnival and ensures that the successful second life of the people remains intact.

The criminalisation process then is that cultural process whereby those with power come to define and shape dominant forms of social life and give them specific meanings. More importantly, it is the way that the powerful have the ability to define both how and what we see and, in so doing, the manner in which we perceive the social behaviour of others. They define what is a perversion and therefore what is deemed deviant and what is deemed criminal. Their power passes through the processes of the law to define what are acceptable pleasures and pastimes and those that are forbidden, outlawed, made criminal. Culture is at work when young black men are criminalised for 'DWB: Driving while Black' (Gates 1995) or we contemplate the process whereby 'the rich get rich and the poor get prison'. The powerful also define through culture what music is criminal and what is not; where and when it is played and where not; where we should paint and what; where we should walk and when; what is erotic and not.

We need to start, then, from the proposition that all crime is grounded in culture and simply cannot stand outside of it as an entity of its own with its own existence and life, emanating as it does from the very font of human experience and lived life. However, within this distinction that crime is predominantly concerned with the cultural, we can separate out further particular forms of culture and cultural practices that contain within them resistant themes, dislocations or oppositional formations that are an affront to the dominant processes of power and therefore must become defined as criminal. That is, cultural behaviour that in some way confronts the processes of power. Whilst Mayor Rudy Giuliani waged his war on 'smut' in New York by closing down its strip clubs, actress Nicole Kidman posed naked every night for theatre audiences in David Hare's play *The Blue Room* and was hailed as a great actress giving a great performance by titillated theatre critics. Yet art photographer Spencer Turnick was arrested and charged with organising an unlawful assembly in New York after coaxing 150 citizens to strip naked for a group portrait in Times Square. In England the Vice-Chancellor of the University of Central England faced criminal prosecution under the Obscene Publications Act for 12 months, for daring to keep the work of photographer Robert Mapplethorpe, with its challenging images of sexuality, in the library of his university.

The theft of private property itself presupposes the existence of the social and economic organisation of private property along with the cultural practices that support it. As such, theft is an act that challenges both the economic and social organisation of life and its culture and so must be criminalised. The act of theft is not necessarily thought through or intended but it is a challenge nevertheless that has to be met and responded to in some way by the powerful themselves. It is not too difficult to imagine a scenario where such acts of theft could be defined as right. Indeed film plots such as that of *The Dirty Dozen* have long romanticised a situation whereby criminals are let loose to be criminal on behalf of the State.

Occasionally, however, theft becomes an intentional challenge to the dominant values of law and order, as in the case in New Orleans in 1896 when Homer Plessey passed himself off as 'white' and sat in the 'whites only' section of a tram. The courts ruled that he had illegally 'passed himself off' as being white, he had stolen 'whiteness', stolen the property and culture of others and so had challenged the existing rule of law (Diamond 1996).

What is erotic and what is obscene and deemed criminal are daily defined by dominant desires. Orderly and acceptable social behaviour stands superior to the disorderly and anti-social. In a life organised around the rationality of science, creativity and culture carry within them the challenge of the criminal. Transgressive crime stands separately from resistant crime in that transgression is an act that breaks through boundaries in order to shock and stand outside of the existing rules, regulations and rhythms of the social world. To resist is both to challenge yet change from within the existing boundaries. There is nothing unique in the oppositional characteristics of cultural practices. It is the fact that culture continually challenges, disrupts and carnivalises the serious business of 'order' that in itself becomes a threat to law and order. This opposition comes from all directions, challenging all the nooks and crannies of 'order' and in that sense all culture is political. The very act of criminalising culture politicises culture.

Pleasure, leisure and desire become central to non-work life whilst the disorder of destruction becomes in itself a 'delight' to be sought and savoured (Katz 1988). A field of fresh virgin snow presents us with a challenge as we delight in being the first to destroy it. The destruction of course is transient and the challenge of destruction will come again with the next fall of snow. Or as Deleuze (1997: 27) notes, 'Destruction is merely the reverse of creation and change, disorder is another form of order and the decomposition of death is equally the composition of life'. Order (and therefore disorder) is a cultural phenomenon that art challenges and, by doing so, itself becomes criminalised. Order is the destruction of art and art the destruction of order. Mapplethorpe's images confuse 'order' by the situating of his sexually explicit representations within an acceptable artistic framework. So his image 'Perfect Moment', mounted in the Cincinnati art gallery, was found by the courts to have enough 'formal properties' to outweigh the evidence of 'obscenity'. This is a nicety that seems to have eluded the West Midlands police in their handling of the arrest of the Vice-Chancellor of the Central England University.

Much performance art further challenges the distinction between art and crime by using pornography stars and prostitutes as the stage on which the politics of the body is enacted. The 'Deep inside Porn Stars' and Annie Sprinkle's 'Post Porn Modernism' (1989) shows in the USA and the work of Maggie O'Neill with 'working girls' in Stoke-on-Trent in May 1999 are good examples of this. Sprinkle talks of her performance not as illegal and criminal but as something with an entirely different understanding of the meaning of prostitution.

> Everyone in the audience gets a rattle which they shake while I breathe, undulate and masturbate myself with a vibrator into an exotic trance, often to a full bodied and clitoral orgasm. It is a ritual originating from the ancient sacred prostitutes, which I recreate on stage. It is these moments in which I feel most powerful; a shaman/witch/healer capable of visions.
>
> (Cited in Schneider 1997: 58)

Here the prostitute is the producer, the commodity and the seller in a domain seeped in criminality which is both challenged and confused by the notion of the performance of art. (Benjamin 1973: 171). Artist J. S. G. Boggs is well known for his drawings of bank notes, which he uses as currency to pay for bills. He has been pursued by authorities on both sides of the Atlantic on charges of counterfeiting, yet he argues that his art is worth more than the bills he pays them with (Weschler 1999). Ten years ago the Bank of England took him to court for counterfeiting, where he was acquitted by the 'sympathetic' jury. Here again culture confuses the categorisation of criminality. At other times the sense of the macabre in art 'revolts' polite society too much, as in the case of Anthony-Noel Kelly's death art, when he was imprisoned for stealing parts of the human body to make sculptures with. He continued his 'body art' when released with his next exhibition 'Birthdays', which involved the mass photographing of 168 naked men and women taken at every age from birth to death safely positioned once more within the parameters of both the dominant art form and, as a consequence, the law.

There is then a hidden aesthetic in the disorderly which results in what Katz describes as the 'delight in being deviant' (Katz 1988: 312). This takes us to the very edge of the challenge of crime and the breaking of boundaries that lie at the heart of both transgression and crime (see Foucault 1977; Lyng 1990; Ferrell and Hamm 1998). When Katz links criminal acts with aesthetics he rightly identifies the construction of criminal culture and style; with style being essentially the grammar of display and with performance becoming an essential element of crime in the same way that the performance of carnival becomes the performance of disorder. The process of resisting through the performance of protestation has always proved uncomfortable for those in authority, with the 'clown' as a cultural form deemed deviant as a breaker of rules and as such a challenge to authority. As all teachers know, the class clown is where any challenge to order will come from, with the clown's internal dynamic of disruption, disorder and dissent presenting a different logic in a world turned upside-down.

Everyday life, culture and crime

If nothing else our everyday lives are the minute-by-minute creation of our own realities. It is the bringing together of meanings and meaning-making into the practices of social life that becomes the very font of culture and cultural forms and therefore crime. We make ourselves and our worlds through our life experiences in a way that appears transparent to both us and the outside world, yet it is in reality nothing more than our daily lives in motion. Every day we have to make sense of senseless lives, often resulting in what appear to others to be senseless criminal acts. We are confronted every day with questions about the world we make: why we are poor or rich; why we work or don't; why we do domestic work or don't; why others talk to us or not. What we desire, enjoy or are excited by all circulate in the micro-circuitry of our thoughts and perceptions, continually interacting with the thoughts and micro-responses of others and other cultural forms that surround us. This passing of our social life is the passing of both time and history and is life that cannot be lived again but only analysed, categorised and passed into 'official' history by others, where it becomes 'obvious', taken for granted and emptied of struggle, structure, pain and passion. History forms no structured 'whole' yet is made to appear as if it does by those with the power to do so; in this way and as such both they and history are empowered with seemingly 'natural' authority. It is through these processes that the meanings of crime become lost, buried deep in the histories of the powerful where crime becomes reprocessed into the discourse of evil acts and evil people.

Yet the activities and performance of everyday life create rich meanings in both abstract and concrete forms which are as abstract and complex as any verbal language. The old military offence of 'dumb insolence' was an affront to 'good order', its sullen sneer to authority contained within it description, analysis and criticism of both structural power and the practices of power which made it indeed a threat to 'good order' and therefore the military equivalent of a criminal offence. Here performance contains within it abstraction and analysis in a lived form that has become necessary to us all in the very continuance and reproduction of our humanity. How else could we live with oppression and knowing that we are oppressed? We are none of us passive beings blindly and instinctively plodding through a life we do not begin to think about or don't want to think about, like some mindless unknowing bird or animal, not knowing why we do this or do that (Elias 1991). The cuckoo does not 'know' why it vandalises the nests of others, but those of us who destroy or vandalise social and private property are not burdened by instinct in the same way. We understand but may not have at our disposal a language or a discourse which can make real sense of our actions to others and privilege them with real historical understandings.

> Mainly our aggression came through language that was either hurled abundantly and defiantly at all that controlled us, or withheld totally, creating a passive silence, that built a wall of non-communication. There was nothing quite like a silent sneer as an answer to interrogation, to provoke instant wrath and punishment; and when that happened they knew they had failed in their attempts to hide their control, their power. The relationship between

us was brought suddenly and very fully out in the open where we played our part and they theirs. The real violence came later, after the school years were finished and when we were old enough to drink. Then we would set out to invite violence, revel in it and mixed with music, almost dance to it. It was then, later, that I lost bits of teeth and gathered scars and hit a few heads, getting barred and thrown out of shops, pubs, cinemas and dance halls; and one summer in 1964 managed to find myself in the queue outside the camp manager's office at Butlin's holiday camp to be removed for fighting.

(Presdee 1988)

We are all aware where we stand in relation to others as we pass through social space. We know what it is that we do but also know that the discourse of diagnosis about our actions is formed not by us but by others. We are judged both by them and by ourselves, using differently created criteria formed from different cultural contexts. We are all social scientists in that sense: we analyse those we mingle with and comment on how they live their lives. It is life as 'soap opera' with the data of life being classified minute by minute as we form ourselves and learn to be poor and learn to be subordinate and, above all, learn to be criminal.

Yet our lives are made sense of by other more dominant and seemingly rational logics that propose that the lives of the subordinate are simply non-cultural, deviant and pathological. This supposed rational world is one where meaning is forever created from information that is also being forever created and also forever and conveniently forgotten. That is, new understandings and knowledges are continually created as old understandings and knowledges are continually discarded. It is these knowledges that make sense of what we do, that categorise our actions as criminal or not, as transgressions of boundaries drawn by others and deemed by them to be deviant and disorderly. Indeed, breaking through the constraints created for us by others becomes a crime in itself, with culture providing for us the social sites for popular transgressions. There is a logic that overarches modern everyday life and that is the overwhelming logic of transgression. There can be no more exciting way of doing 'edge-work' (Lyng 1990) for the 'law-abiding' than 'lawbreaking'. Transgressing takes us to the very edge of 'lawfulness', where we stand and stare into the canyon of 'lawlessness'. It takes us to the edge of all that is approved of and defined as respectable. It carries the threat of being sent into social oblivion tantalisingly held before us, with its accompanying promise of a life as an outsider, to be dominated by the degradation of the rejected. We are confronted by the challenge of being lawless every day as we gamble, play with and push to the limits the fine line between order and disorder. The more successful the gamble becomes, the more heightened becomes the associated pleasure.

The culture of everyday life 'delivers' our actions to the door of the dominant expressions of right and wrong for judgement, thereby beginning the process of cultural criminalisation. Graffiti is destruction; the oil painting is art. Cockfighting is cruel; hunting is rural culture. Glyndebourne celebrates classical music outdoors and is 'cultural'; rave music performed outdoors which emits 'sounds wholly or predominantly characterised by the emission of a succession of repetitive beats' (Criminal Justice and Law and Order Act 1994) is criminal. To consent to violence in 'hate' is sport; to consent to violence in 'love' is a crime. To be affluent is to be worthy; to be impoverished and in debt is a crime. The criminalisation of culture is no more than the legalisation of prejudice and moral beliefs held by the powerful over and against the powerless, the poor and the dispossessed.

There is then a need for cultural criminology to examine both the cultural contradictions of contemporary society from which criminalised culture emanates. It also needs to examine the dynamics of a consumer culture that demands the irrationality of the commodification of more and more of social life that stands alongside an economic system that demands more and more order and rationality.

Consumption and crime

For crime to come into 'being' and to enter the realm of popular consciousness there must exist a tentative arrangement between criminal, police, media and the public on the criminalising process. The car 'joyrider' does not come into 'being' until chased by the police. The popular knowledge of the passion of 'joyriding' is then contextualised into culture by the media and transposed into popular consciousness by the public. All have their place and part to play in the process of the construction and the definition of crime and, as such, all become true partners in crime (Ferrell 1996). In this way the police, the public and the media are as much a part of the process of crime as the person identified and defined as the criminal. When Sartre interviewed Jean Genet about his earlier life, Genet remarked:

> It is the criminal who creates the police, and it is the police who create the criminal ... I decided to be what crime made of me ... I think the word 'thief' wounded me deeply. Deeply, that is to say, to make me want to be it [a thief] proudly and in spite of them.
>
> (Genet quoted in Sartre 1963: 71)

In this way the powerless put into place the last link in the logic of being powerless by doing what is expected of them by both the powerful and the powerless. It is an attempt to bring about the inevitable consequences of social power in the same way that Hebdige talks about facial tattooing as a way of 'throwing yourself away before they do it for you' (Hebdige 1988: 32).

In that sense only the individual knows why they acted in a such a way that to others appears to be an inevitable result of social structures. Genet also described this logic of transgressing when he described how pirates actively placed themselves outside of society:

> In days of old, on the galley, pirates had those frightful

ornaments all over their body so that life in society became impossible for them. Having willed that impossibility themselves, they suffered less from the rigour of fate. They willed it, limited their universe in its space and comfort.

(Genet quoted in Brain 1979: 159–160)

When the media enter the realm of crime it is the commodification process that is at work with the dynamics of the communications marketplace being the driving force. Consumption and communication come together to form the engine room of criminalisation. Modern media forms suggest to us that the social world cannot be grasped directly but needs to be specially mediated into a world of immediacy, so that all acts become instant and devoid of memory. The mediation of memory becomes the mediation of history itself, with the role of the media and consumption being to prioritise immediacy and eradicate popular memory. In immediacy speed, that is time, is all as process becomes invisible; must become invisible and disappear. We no longer have 'lives' but a 'life', in the present, as the micro-circuitry of culture is transmitted through the cultural conduit of the media into the wider cultural matrices of everyday life (Websdale 1998). In this way not only is crime mediated by the media but the audience of society consumes information about crime from which it forms a popular conception of crime that, in turn, becomes part of popular ahistorical knowledge. All that is left of crime is excitement and desire as crime itself becomes transposed into a commodity. As an economic and social system, capitalism worries little about what is or is not commodified. It operates free from the vagaries of morality, preferring instead the more scientific and rational approach of its 'central imperatives' of 'expansion, realisation of surplus value, profit', which 'ensures a certain indifference to the terrain it's working on and through' (Weeks 1985: 21).

This commodification of social life becomes the process whereby all social relations and 'sociability' come to be seen in terms of use-value and therefore exchange value. Consequently social life, and therefore crime, become both a fetish and a commodity. The drive to have or appear to have, that is to consume, becomes the nightmare of a post-modern society, imprisoning and corralling all of society into the consumption process. Here two elements are at play. First, crime is created and presented as a commodity to the communications market. Second, a process as all-inclusive as consumption will always hold within it the potential for transgression. Transgression and crime thereby become a cultural necessity, if not a given, of everyday modern life.

The dynamics of modern marketing have further created the notion of niche marketing and consumption, which further isolate us not only from each other but from a holistic and integrated way of life. Now we can watch just animals on specialist television channels, buy magazines just about animals, buy T-shirts with animals on and indeed live a life of 'just animals'. We distil these cultural isolatories and ingest them as everyday life. Through modern marketing methods and with the help of the globalisation of communications through the Internet, the micro becomes magically the macro. We can, through consumption, live out our hidden desires as life itself. The bizarre becomes normalised, de-fantasised, real. We can live a life of crime or violence or can choose to saturate ourselves in sex through cybernetics. In the same way that the 'money' game Monopoly injects fun and fantasy into the harsh world of monopoly capitalism, thereby emptying it of its essential conflicts, contradictions and politics, so the media have appropriated the politics of 'law and order' for their own ends and reconstructed it as a meaningless form of popular culture. In this new world crime and disorder take on the new imperatives and dynamics of the processes of production and consumption of commodities; they thereby become imbued with new meanings.

The pleasure of crime

At the heart of the relationship between commodification, consumption and culture is the heightened pursuit of pleasure, which has become the necessary lubricant of everyday consumer life. We all have to desire to consume in order to survive socially. The resulting pleasure we experience must be both uplifting and temporary, giving us a glancing cultural 'high' that will return us to the doors of desire, once again ready and eager for more consumption. Emotionality rather than rationality becomes an important element of popular culture as we seek to 'feed' our 'need' through the pursuit of 'danger, pleasure and excitement' (Ferrell and Hamm 1998). This pursuit of popular pleasure contained within a culture of consumption becomes a continuing problem for legislators and moral reformers who endeavour to manage pleasure through legislation and control mechanisms that attempt to define particular desires and pleasures as deviant and criminal. But there is, and has been in the past, a lack of any understanding of the dynamics of pleasure itself. No sooner have the powerful punished the 'pleasured' then punishment itself becomes a pleasure and weaves its way back into everyday life. In this way leisure, pleasure and excitement become inextricably entwined into popular culture and everyday life. Once handcuffs were a sign of oppression by authority, signifying the imprisonment of the body. Now handcuffs are a fashion accessory available up and down the high street, signifying a form of sexual pleasure. Much crime is masochistic in nature in the sense that to be punished for one's transgressions is a demonstration of the law's absurdity. The 'you must not do that' becomes 'you have to do that'. Crime and receiving punishment can both be acts of rebellion. As Reik (1962: 145, 163) suggests, punishment shows an 'invincible rebellion, demonstrating that he gains pleasure despite the discomfort . . . he cannot be broken from outside. He has an inexhaustible capacity for taking a beating and yet knows unconsciously he is not licked'. Not to punish breaks this contract and confuses, leading to further transgression. It is a no-win situation for the forces of 'order' because 'disorder' is in part defined by punishment.

I was often punished. It was something we expected,

invited, almost demanded. At school I was caned for writing out a betting slip during Latin, using a copy of the *Daily Mirror* racing page for the details. I'm not sure whether it was the betting slip or the *Daily Mirror* that incensed the teacher but I remember the long walk to the Deputy Head's office and his talk of educating generations of Presdee's and how it was sad it had come to this, and shouldn't I be ashamed. But I wasn't, and afterwards, when I walked out, I smiled at the Latin teacher who stood and witnessed it all. I went to the 'Jet and Whittle' that lunch time and passed the bet in the toilet; they wouldn't stop me.

(Presdee 1988)

It is in this world of ever-increasing commodification that we are now situated and where seemingly irrational acts of destruction and violence intermingle with pleasure, fun, desire and performance. With the rational imperatives of economic life held over and against us, we respond with irrational emotions derived from desire, pleasure and the sensualness of a post-modern commodity culture. It is a world full of contradictions, inequalities and struggle, yet it is a world where, as Freud recognised, the pursuit of pleasure is potentially antagonistic to the State (Freud 1955).

When punishment becomes a desired outcome, to be worn as a medal to demonstrate our ability to 'riot for pleasure', then legislators become impotent in their struggle for law and order. Here the carnivalesque becomes a challenge to both the law and the lawmaker, with the creation of the 'world upside down' no longer being the exclusive domain of carnival, as the debasing of the dominant symbolic system now fragments into the social events of everyday life. Bakhtin (1984), in his study of carnival, saw the potential for the transgressive characteristics of carnival to become incorporated into other social sites such as subversive literature. By this process popular culture becomes carnivalesque by nature and thereby transmutes into the 'world upside-down' in a lived form. Old orders and rationalities appear irrational as contemporary culture emphasises emotion over education. In Australia a chip shop owner becomes a leader of a political party. In our newspapers motor experts 'philosophise' on cars. In Britain a bus conductor becomes an author and we can all be chefs and wine experts, film and music makers. As carnival itself becomes 'festivalised' and appropriated as a commodity and separated from the context of popular protest, so the social prerequisites for the carnival of crime come into being. Truth and falsity become interposed as falsity becomes reality for all and lawmakers try desperately to make sense of the senseless world of commodities. In this world there can be no sense but only pleasure in a world where theft, and even cruelty and violence, can be satiated by the consumption of cultural forms provided by the media and the pleasure industry.

Put simply, transgressing and doing wrong are for many an exciting and pleasurable experience. For others to be involved in some way in the act of transgression as a voyeur is pleasure enough. To watch, to be there yet absent, is enough. We know that to watch and enjoy pain, violence, cruelty and crime, is transgressing in itself and produces both pleasure and guilt. A global multimedia industry enables us to consume many of these forbidden pleasures in the privacy of our own homes without questioning how these commodities come into being or whether there are victims involved. In a sense others do our crime for us and the multimedia deliver the pleasures to us via the Internet and a growing 'reality' television. We can watch in secret without the disapproving 'gaze' of the ordered, rational world of authority. The very individuality created by capitalism contains within it the heart of transgression, but hidden from view, unseen and unknown. The old notion that we need to police and regulate the borders between the public and the private domains is now receding into the need to police the 'individual', no matter where they socially reside. When these hidden transgressive thoughts move from the private to the public, they often do so in an extravaganza of violence and crime and the 'debris' of carnival takes over.

3 From carnival to the carnival of crime

(With Gavin Carver)

In the autumn when darkness begins to descend earlier and earlier, the sound and flashes of fireworks exploding in the distance begin to herald the coming of Bonfire Night. Each year on 5 November, a festival of fire and fireworks is celebrated throughout Britain that literally lights up the country in a veritable carnival of noise and destruction that excites all classes and all ages. When I was a youth I watched with increasing excitement as people piled old furniture, boxes and all manner of possessions into colourful mountains that I knew we would soon be allowed to destroy by fire. It is a celebration that not long ago was held in back gardens or at the end of streets but now takes place at official public venues such as parks or school grounds. Whereas once as participants we felt close to the force of the fire and destruction, so now we are distanced as mere spectators. Once it was a night of transgression, danger and disorder but now it is commercially sponsored, regulated and ordered.

At the same time that we have civilised and sanitised Bonfire Night, so the incidence of arson is on the increase with school buildings often the target. Now when cars are stolen they are often paraded, performed with and ceremoniously burnt. In the French city of Lyons more than 1,000 cars were burnt in 1998 whilst the 'sport' of fire-bombing attendant firemen prompted the banning of sales of petrol in containers to young people under the age of 18 years. All this was explained by sociologist Farhad Khosrokhavar: 'When firemen put out a car that is burning they stop the show that people are enjoying as a break from their daily lives' (*The Times* 27/4/99). In the north-east of England the district of Tyne and Wear has over 30,000 illegal fires a year, mostly the work of young people who target the oppressive institutions of their lives (namely schools and bad housing). Meanwhile in America the Burning Man fire festival celebrates the creativity of destruction in a feast of flames as 25,000 people of all ages descend on the desert to transgress through an orgasm of pyro-fetishism, bringing together both carnival and crime. The question that we need to explore is how have we moved from carnival to crime; from carnival to the carnival of crime.

Carnival is a much used and abused term, but it is none the less the most appropriate frame within which to discuss the performance of excitement and transgression with which this book is most concerned. Let's overcome one hurdle at the start. The transgressive excitements of carnival performances are not assumed to be all positive; nor am I proposing that all artefacts of popular cultures and countercultures are pleasurable. In the ecstatic, marginal, chaotic acts of carnival, damage is done, people are hurt and some 'pleasurable' performances reflect on or articulate pain. In other words carnival can be both violent and break the law. The film *Trainspotting* is an example of these complex engagements, where the consumption of the film may well be in part enjoyable (it is 'well' written, 'well' directed, etc.) yet it depicts a world that is ambivalent in its attitude to the cause and effect of pain. The film neither demonises nor glorifies the use of heroin: at times the lives shown are full of pleasure, at times that pleasure is shown to have a dear price. The consumption of the film is as complex as the content. Here there is an artefact of popular culture, depicting an act of counterculture showing neither to be easily boxed.

Carnival then is the ritualised mediation between order and disorder *par excellence*, furthermore it is a domain in which the pleasure of playing at the boundaries (social and personal) is most clearly provided for. Within the period of carnival the negotiations between the powerful and the people, as previously described, are ritually rehearsed, not however in the debating chamber but in the streets (or the social domain), and not with solemnity but laughter, however cruel.

Our purpose here is to explore the excitement and cultural necessity of carnival in everyday life and further to explore how in a post-modern society it is no longer enough to 'do' carnival once, twice or three times a year. Under the 'unbearable' rationality of modern life, acts of carnival become a daily need for social survival. I do not propose that carnival can be taken as an explanatory cosmology for all the acts described. However, I do suggest that carnival (as a performed event and as a critical discourse) is one way to interrogate these acts, a paradigm by which performed acts of excess and excitement may be discussed. Furthermore it is possible to use theories of carnival, and examples from carnival's history, to critique aspects of our contemporary culture.

The carnival we know

Popular, participatory, indulgent or transgressive festivities have been performed by cultures throughout recorded history. While this is not a chapter on cultural or ritual history, it is necessary to remind ourselves of the breadth and depth of these excessive performances, to appreciate fully the central role that these occasions played in the way that communities regulated themselves and identified themselves.

Probably the first recorded carnival, although not of course going by that name, was the Egyptian festival of Osiris. This was celebrated in a designated 'time out of time', five days that were seen as outside of the traditional calendar – and being outside of ordinary time, they were host to behavioural codes outside of the norm. Osiris, who was born on the first of the five days, having been murdered and dismembered by his brother, was revived by his sister Isis, and became lord of the dead. The celebration of Osiris was thus a festivity of birth, death and rebirth, held in the passage of winter to spring; it thus represented a seasonal rebirth. The festival itself – involving procession, animal and genital imagery, effigies of Osiris and ritual sacrifice – was in part a ritual of fertility and rebirth, a plea for the revival of the land and reinvigoration of the people.

We may now all know more about the passage of the earth through the sky, but our remaining seasonal festivities (few and lamentable though many are) still aim to revive our souls in the dark of winter in preparation for the new cycle. Of course, winter is now less potent: we can work and be kept warm and fed in winter, so we need to ask where our down-times are that need to be filled with such festive pleasures. The answer, I suggest, is that in a world which is daily 'down', there is a daily need for festive pleasures and a daily need for carnival. As Durkheim clearly points out, the isolation of modern individualism can only be compensated for by separating out 'effervescence' from daily (everyday) life (Durkheim 1982). The five days of Osiris are with us now all the time, on bank holidays, the weekend, Friday nights, girls' nights out. In an organised industrial society based on rationality, efficiency and effectiveness, the 'down times' become a daily part of everyday life and the need for the carnivalesque becomes a part of it.

The Greek festival of Dionysus, mythologically complex though it is, had at its heart celebrations of the vine, of feasting and of liberated, violent and ecstatic physical performance. Symbolised by the bull and the (dismembered) phallus, Dionysus has come to symbolise the complexity of pleasure *par excellence*. He is paradoxical; his nature is that he represents both joy to the world and savage madness. He is god of the vine as source of fruit, pleasure and intoxication. Although represented by a phallus, he is separated from it, and rather than the god of birth (although born twice), he is the god of eruption and appearance.

In ancient Rome the two festivals of Kalends and Saturnalia are recorded as clearly exhibiting performances of excess and transgression. Masking, often as animals, was central to these (and most other) festivals, taking on the mythological and actual facets of these 'natural' creatures. At Saturnalia slaves were temporarily freed and were served on by their masters (although the universality of this practice is open to debate). Feasting, sex, combat, games, pranks, fruits of the land, sacrifice and mockery were then all important ritual elements, variously performed throughout a festival period that occupied a significant part of the winter. Seneca describes this as a period of indulgence, hedonism and transgression from the norm. We must be careful of course not to essentialise these performances, it is too easy to use the distance of history to frame these events with a simple narrative of indulgence and fertility ritual, universally celebrated. Within any of these performance texts we must assume complex layers of levels and intentions of involvement. The symbolic motivation and components of many aspects are unclear or debated, and sources are questionable. Moreover while it is clear that elements of the ritual allude to the power of magic, one must presume that its observance was as much down to its social power and its role as carnal rejuvenator in a time out of time.

Carnival and Christianity

These festivals of magical and social ritual, of worship and subversion, pleasure and violence, existed in cultures across Europe, ritualising the relationship of humanity and nature, providing a structure of myth and expression to articulate a communal vision of the order, and disorder, of things. The emergent mono-deism and religious tolerance of Christianity sought to incorporate these festivals into its own ritual structure, attempting to contain what was seen as a threatening and pagan set of values while still providing contexts for celebration. The need for carnival was accepted and to some extent tolerated as a senseless time full of senseless irrational acts that appeared necessary, even 'natural', in the rhythm of the year.

The few lines above do not do justice to the centuries of complex cultural negotiation between Church and people, the former seeking in various ways to facilitate the traditional celebrations of the latter while ensuring the dominance of the Christian orthodoxy. Dionysian and carnal revelry, turning the world upside down, did not sit comfortably with a faith in one merciful but moral God. This process is nowhere more clear than in the manipulation of the event now known as carnival, and the associated festivities of the Feast of Fools. Although the precise origin of the term carnival is unknown, it is likely that its root lies in *carne vale* (farewell to the flesh), and specifically referred to the period of festive excess, particularly the feasting on meat, prior to Lent. It also refers to a more general indulgence in carnality before the Lenten fast. The festival itself varies across time and countries but is effectively a ritual of indulgence, reversal, performance, mockery and excess. The Church initially sought to challenge and ban these rites, but the momentum of popular belief, coupled undoubtedly with the appeal of the festival, made eradication or full metamorphosis impossible and indeed unwise. By the Middle Ages carnival had found its way into the activities and calendar of the Church, involving congregations and clergy in rites of excess and reversal, processions, feasts and performances, partly intertwined with festivals that the Church had appropriated from various pre-Christian rituals: the Feast of Fools was celebrated in the twelve days from Christmas to Epiphany, and carnival prior to Lent. The Church made moves to rid itself of the excesses of such festivals, while keeping many of the more acceptable trappings of the festivals, in part as a demonstration of its tolerance advocated by some of its members. Consequently, in the Renaissance and early modern period elements of rites of reversal and excess survived within the Church, having come to be taken as an essential and natural part of religious festivals, while other aspects had been removed to more marginal arenas of social performance.

Capitalism and carnival

It is not only institutions such as Church and State that have sought to appropriate or control popular festivity. Elements of carnival were commercialised or appropriated by the well-intentioned middle classes and the rationalising project of modernism. In these cases local processions, fire festivals or fairs came to be organised not by 'the people' but by respectable societies or businessmen, the former with the intention of providing acceptable entertainment, often promoting good causes, the latter offering the same but in the pursuit of profit. (This is problematic, of course, since the 'people' are not one body.) Examples range from the development of Blackpool pleasures as an industrial reworking of carnival (Formations Collective 1983) to the still extant village and town pageants as well-intentioned and edifying (however empty) reworkings. Equally, elements of the carnivalesque naturally appeared in cultural output such as theatre, and with the advent of printing, cartoons and chapbooks. These forms also served to promote folk customs in general, but in the printed presentation of the material it has been argued that much of its vigorous, vernacular and topical quality was lost.

Fiske (1991) has provided a number of examples of the legislative and cultural containment of popular festive practices in the nineteenth century. These he allies closely to the fear of the bourgeoisie at losing their control over the working classes, and in an attempt to assert their control they sought to contain or condemn those leisure pursuits they deemed unfitting or undesirable. Such activities were perhaps condemned due to their disturbance of local highways, or their cruelty and non-productivity, but underneath there was always the realisation that the Dionysian behaviour of 'the other' both threatened and challenged because it did not fit in with a set of values that sustained the middle classes. Cunningham also illustrates the appropriation of the lower-class street game of football by the middle classes, controlling and containing its whirling quasi-violent nature. Now once more we see the carnival in football re-emerge not on the field but on the terraces (Armstrong 1994).

The point of this brief history is to illustrate the pervasiveness of transgressive performances throughout previous cultures, and more particularly to exemplify the complex relationship that these performances had with the dominant order; critical, potentially threatening, but in the end necessary and thus a target for appropriation and manipulation. Here it is the 'necessary' quality that forms the focus of my analysis of contemporary deviant and criminal behaviour.

Theoretical background

The most important analysis of the nature of carnival, and the one that has been drawn upon most frequently by modern cultural critics, is that of the work of Mikhail Bakhtin, who writes of a set of values and behaviours found in the works of Rabelais. Bakhtin has often been cited and paraphrased, and it is with caution that I do so here. Nevertheless, an outline of his work (and others who came after) is necessary to contextualise the theoretical base with which this text approaches the idea of carnival.

What then are the constituent elements of carnival? What is it that has been extracted by contemporary cultural theorists to use as an analytical paradigm for social/cultural behaviour in the late twentieth century? Carnival was a time of great festive excess where the pleasures of the 'body' were foregrounded, in opposition to the dominant and accepted values of restraint and sobriety. Contained within this excess is the notion of transgression that is so central to the operation of carnival. Through its acts, structure and imagery, carnival legitimates its participants' behaviour. This behaviour would, outside of carnival, be considered to be outside the norm, and beyond the bounds of propriety as judged within the 'normal' social space and calendar of everyday life. Intimately connected with acts of transgression is the upturning or reversal of dominant authority structures. Carnival licenses transgression and thus openly defies or mocks the values of the hegemony. The transgressor is thereby put in a position of power as the carnival society temporarily replaces the dominant one. Examples of these acts are legion: boys become bishops and give sermons; the fool becomes king; mock processions and crownings are held; the prices of foods are reversed; slaves become masters; and the normally private functions of the body become objects of popular laughter. Officers 'wait' on the men at Christmas; men wait on women (here I am thinking of the rituals of Mother's Day). On 'rag' days students throw bags of flour at the police and generally enjoy disorder without sanction. It is truly the 'world upside down', full of irrational, senseless, offensive behaviour – a time of disorder and transgression and of doing wrong in an ordered world. In other words, carnival sanctions enjoyable behaviour that in the ordered world we would often accept as criminal.

Bakhtin's writing places much emphasis on the body, most particularly on the grotesque body. In this sense he sees carnival as a celebration of the connectedness of the body to the world: through ingestion and excretion, birth and death, the grotesque constantly reminds us that we are not separated from Nature's cycle; we are not closed off and 'above' our natural context but are inherently part of it. Thus carnival celebrates orifices and sex organs, extreme youth and age, sex, stomachs, birth and death. Through this emphasis on change, carnival reminds us that though we are mortal the laughing human spirit is immortal, since we die, are returned to the earth and nurture further life. This position is wholly opposed to the sobriety of the classical body, separated from the process of life. Carnival, in its language and imagery, is not afraid of the 'arse hole', the 'prick' or the 'cunt'. Indeed, as carnival inverts the social structure, so too does it invert the body, for in the carnival universe the head (the location of reason) is uncrowned by the stomach, the genitals and the arse. Faeces and the fart, the burp and the belly laugh all become an integral part of the logic and language of carnival. The performance of carnival uses the body as the stage, claiming it back from those who wish to control it, who wish to appropriate that which it produces, to civilise it, or even imprison it. Carnival places the body in a trance-like state where, like the carnival of rave, one can 'play with one's body and carry out a state of enthusiasm . . . near to the happy state of mind' (Jeanmaire 1951: 58). Now Artaud's 'festival of the street' takes the people not only out of their bodies but in so doing out of society into a state of ecstasy.

In the same vein carnival revels in abuse. Using popular argot, it brings down the mighty and uses language, the tool of discourse and reason, as a celebration of oaths, of colloquial language and abuse. The many popular unofficial voices of carnival shout in opposition to the monologic speech of the dominant order. Against the coherent logic and language of the talking head, the stomach and the arse speak out the belch and the fart, destroying the logic of language and in its way disrupting and destroying order. The carnivalesque becomes the language of disrespect *par excellence* for, after all, carnival is not a spectacle seen by the people but lived by them (Bakhtin 1984: 37).

Thus carnival represents a world upside down, but most importantly a world that is restructured through laughter, for alongside its images of social upheaval carnival is joyful. The laughter comes, as Eco *et al.* (1984) point out, through the breaking of a rule, and this laughter is both deriding and revitalising, ambivalent or Janus-faced. Additionally the laughter is both directed out to those in authority and is self-reflexive; carnival laughs at itself while it laughs at others. Its laughter appeals, as Orwell remarked in 'The Art of Donald McGill', to the 'Unofficial self, the voice of the belly protesting against the soul' (Orwell 1941: 144). Humour rightly understands the law, its weaknesses and its true lack of rationality. It truly transcends the law and carnival humour looks to the consequences. Here in carnival is the 'survival' humour of Nuttall and Carmichael (1977) which challenges and contests, turns inside-out and upside-down the efforts of authority to maintain law and order. Crime is here the subversion of bourgeois order.

Since authority structures are challenged and overturned, it is possible to perceive carnival as the voice of those below, those on the social margins. More properly though carnival must be seen as multivocal, since the last thing that the contingent and shifting authority of carnival attempts to do is unify or polarise. Neither are the victims of carnival only those who wield power. The carnival body may terrorise (actually and metaphorically) the weak as much as the strong, the oppressed as much as the oppressors. Rather than offering a fixed, albeit reversed position, the world view offered by carnival seems to question the supremacy of any authority, replacing it with relativity and foregrounding the popular and grotesque body above the fixed and static. On a simple level carnival may be seen as a time when low becomes high and vice versa, but more deeply carnival throws into question certain fixed notions of high and low, articulating their questionable status and claim to authority. It is, in other words, the 'counter rites of the masses' (Bouvier 1994).

As a period of licensed misrule, classic carnival is faced with the ultimate closure: Lent must arrive and carnival must end. Thus one line of argument proposes that far from providing a space for the normally disposed to offer an alternative commentary on the world, carnival simply reaffirms the supremacy of the dominant order. Officers go back to being waited on by the 'men', and women go back to waiting on their menfolk. This it does by two means. On the one hand carnival proposes only one alternative to the status quo which is seen as a world of chaos and disorder. On the other hand, where carnival satirises extant power structures, it does so by mimicry, thus finally validating the potency of the hierarchy. We may see a further 'conservative' function of carnival in its ability to unite communities as through communal celebration the people create close ties with their community and effectively celebrate their present identity despite the impositions of the dominant social order (such as the conservative carnival Crews of Old New Orleans, where orders such as the Mistake Crewe of Comes enacted out behind masks the old racist relationships of previous years).

Taken to its furthest extreme, such a position also suggests that through the act of collective mockery and festivity the carnival community exhausts its need for genuine revolution, effectively letting off steam until the next festive season comes around. Although the safety-valve theory hints at conspiracy – that is to say those in power promulgate and promote carnival in order to maintain the status quo – it must also be understood that carnival comes from the 'people' in collusion with the 'State' and that the people are complicit in its closure. This model therefore proposes that carnival is both allowed by those in power in order to maintain harmony, but more significantly the people themselves wish to reaffirm their own position within a harmonious collective existence. Even within the restructured world of carnival, the hierarchical structure of conventional power is recreated and acknowledged to be reversed, thus there is still a ruler and subject, even if the roles are reversed, or the power wielded by the king is seen as ludicrous. Therefore rather than offering an entire alternative structure, carnival offers a distorted reflection of the structure.

The complexity of carnival is that it functions as a playful and pleasurable revolution, where those normally excluded from the discourse of power may lift their voices in anger and celebration, but it also serves as the vindication of the dominant order (and a demonstration of its liberal pluralism as an added bonus). This knife-edge balance, or ambivalence, may work to the benefit of both parties, allowing expression and harmonious reintegration. This balance may therefore be seen as serving the needs of all involved, since as Durkheim (1982) observes, 'harmonious collective life is beneficial to its members'. To say that carnival is either a tool for oppression or a vehicle for potentially subversive expression is too simplistic, since it is both of these things, each articulated through a series of symbolic and cultural actions.

However, there are many moments in the history of carnival where behaviour has broken free of festive restraint and licence and enacted, within the framework of the celebration, a real and violent revolution or rebellion. Examples range from the well-documented riots in the 1580 carnival in

Romans, France, the 1571 May Day celebrations in London and St Giles Fair in Oxford, the anti-Salvation Army demonstrations in Worthing in 1834, and in more modern times the Notting Hill Carnival of 1976. Richard Schechner talks of the violence in American carnival during the turbulence of civil rights protest in the 1960s, when during carnival processions black marchers hurled black and gold painted coconuts 'like cannonballs at white spectators' (Schechner 1993: 74–75). In some of these cases the grievance that caused the violence was exacerbated by the carnival; in others the carnival was used as a mask for the aggressive act. Of course many of the outbreaks of violence were an extreme of festive excess, often responding and in opposition to its imminent closure. Nevertheless, the act of carnival has at its heart a dialectic drama: the people's voice and the display of festive reversal are held against a discourse of normality and restraint; carnival must propose an argument. It is, however, the nature of the event that the argument is rarely transparent or clearly articulated. Instead it is, at least in part, an anti-argument, for rather than making a point through conventional discourse many aspects make their point through lack of discourse. Therefore tied up in any carnival event there may be an underlying social opposition to a hegemonic position, but in the act this argument is rarely apparent. The argument of the body is foregrounded in opposition to that of the head. Ecstasy and laughter versus rationality; Dionysian versus Apollonian. Laughter is not an argument against another but a solution to it, temporarily disempowering the other. It is impossible therefore to see carnival as a strict dialogic opposition but rather as a different way of being, thus an argument without any possible resolution. It is nihilistic or anarchic in nature.

The exploding of carnival in post-modern culture

And so we come to the late twentieth century and the main thrust of the argument. The acceleration of the dominance of capitalism throughout this century coupled with the more cultural aspects of what we have come to term post-modernism have provided the context for a hugely complex fragmentation and reworking of carnival where the debris of carnival litters everyday life. Carnival is no longer a 'parodic reversal' but now a 'true transgression' (Carlson 1996). If this process was in train during the period of rationalism, science and industrialisation, it has become virulent in a period where commodity and consumption are all, and where the idea of the fixed or the authentic has largely become meaningless. Indeed, it is my contention that not only does contemporary mass culture make free use of the idea of carnival in the service of the promotion of excitements, but its very nature is in part carnivalesque. It may be the case that there are very few 'authorised' public performances which are anything but a shadow of Bakhtin's carnival, however the 'second life of the people' is threaded through our culture, often wholly dislocated from the original functions of carnival. It is the nature of carnival to resist containment and closure.

So potent are the excitements of carnival that the pleasure and leisure industries have utilised carnival as a form and as a metaphor, providing commodified carnival experiences and excitements in a variety of contexts, some mainstream, others far more marginal. True to the paradoxical nature of carnival and its apolitical leaning to ecstatic and transgressive pleasures, it does not discriminate whether its articulation is generated from an oppositional or illegal position, or from within legitimate institutions, since part of its operation is to turn the acceptable into the unacceptable and make the unacceptable palatable through joyful humour. In other words carnival laughter and transgressions are as likely to appear in mainstream television (*Spitting Image* or *Blind Date*) (Hunt 1998) as in 'illegal' rave gatherings, Internet sites or joyriding (Fiske 1991; Docker 1996).

Social processes have contrived to suppress carnival in its 'authentic' sense. Demographics and communications have changed the nature of community, and industrial and post-industrial working patterns have removed from the calendar many of the universal points of 'time out of time'. It is increasingly difficult to 'take to the streets' or indeed to 'party'. However, a number of critics have found a wide variety of instances where elements of carnival have emerged in other contemporary forms of social and symbolic activity. It is as if, through the dual processes of scientific rationality and containment, carnival has shattered and its fragments and debris are now to be found in a wide variety of contemporary forms, but hardly ever, ironically, in the remaining shell of what is still called carnival (Stallybrass and White 1986).

Significantly we may be able to take a step back from our own society and see that the very tensions that operate within what we call a post-modern world are the tensions that are central to carnival. Where carnival questions the absolute nature of authority, so does post-modernism; where carnival laughs at 'truth' and order while also laughing at itself, so too does post-modernism. Carnival, like late capitalism, revels in the excitement of consumption, and the media, like carnival, permeates our entire world. Carnival and post-modernism both seem to exist in tension between their critical and conservative functions, but both are finally obsessed with their own contingency: the humorous and the serious; the radical and the conservative – all tensions and paradoxes that are both implicit within carnival and identified time and again within our culture. Carnival, like post-modernism, pays no homage to the author/authority, as texts and artefacts are borrowed and manipulated, contesting the canonical notions of modernity. Culture and ownership of culture are pliant. In the case of post-modernism this plasticity has been variously attributed to the supremacy of consumption, manipulating culture to find the most easily, ecstatically consumable form, a response to (or perhaps boredom with) the great rationalising project of modernism.

It is too easy simply to cite carnival as a 'resistant' form to dominant culture. We must always bear in mind (as Docker [1996] reminds us) that both carnival and our contemporary society are far more complex, and an easy polar position of folk and court cultures is a taxonomy only of convenience. It is possible to suggest that the notions of Court, Church and State have been superseded by the mediating avenues of mass culture, and it is in the relationship between the desire for excessive carnival pleasures and the supply of those pleasures that the carnival tensions exist.

The basic premise of my argument is straightforward: without a partly licensed carnival forum to satisfy our second life, it emerges more haphazardly, unrehearsed and often unannounced. Moreover explosions of carnival into the social field only represent aspects of the carnival; complete carnivals do not (cannot) spontaneously erupt, and if they do they are seen, as Eco *et al.* (1984) note, as riot. Now only elements of carnival erupt, sometimes appearing outside the domain of cultural production and legitimate activity, but sometimes they appear within cultural products. However, by being incomplete they do not manage to balance the paradoxes that Bakhtin's carnival does and without coherence it is relatively easy to separate the unpalatable or savage performances from the acts of pleasant social entertainment.

The question must remain: if carnival bears a resemblance to post-modernism, where are the fragments and debris of carnival in our culture? The list of national and international carnivals that actually exemplify the carnivalesque is slim, and while other celebratory and quasi-authorised events may claim some allegiance to traditional notions of the carnivalesque, it certainly does not appear that the 'second life of the people' has much room for expression in any way that might be formally recognised as a carnival event. There are of course many events called carnival, but most of these are safe, commodified affirmations of dominant values and celebrations of local community and charity rather than times of excess, laughter, reversal and ecstasy. A procession of local charities, a military band, majorettes and a local princess might have the faintest whiff of carnival in its form, but its celebration of high moral values is nothing close to 'the second life of the people'. If these images of carnival are not carnival, then where does the debris of the carnivalesque lie? Where is the 'second life of the people' lived?

We can find elements of carnival in satirical comedy, in novels and films, but here the act has been committed, and the only remaining act of production by the people is the selective and active reading of the carnival texts. It is certainly true that these exist in a complex two-way relationship between reader and producer, and that carnival images in these authored texts are open for appropriation and reworking by more marginal bodies. The fragments that we are interested in here are acts of performance that involve the performers in the production of symbolic and transgressive and sometimes joyful carnival acts.

In the acts of body modification, S&M, raving, recreational drug-taking, hotting and rodeo, gang rituals, the Internet, festivals and extreme sports, lurks the marginal performance of carnival fragments in the late twentieth century. Other acts undoubtedly contain carnival elements; Schechner (1993) and Kershaw (1992) have considered political demonstrations and found them evidencing carnival elements in their performance, but these elements are to a certain extent subsidiary to a greater cause. Similarly many artefacts of mainstream media have been found to demonstrate carnival laughter or carnival resistance; but in these cases the carnival has been appropriated and redelivered; it is, for want of a defining phrase, secondary carnival. These are products of culture and often reflective of culture, but they are not participatory performance acts. These artefacts are a manifestation of carnival desires, and while perhaps not as ersatz or degraded as advertising images, none the less they lack the participation in the pleasures of carnival performance.

Let us be clear about one thing, these events are not carnival in their entirety, nor are they carnival exclusively, but they all contain elements of the performance of pleasure at the margins in opposition to the dominant values of sobriety and restraint. Interestingly these acts are not simply the anomic performances of a dispossessed youth but have become entwined with fashion and performance art, as associated items of counter-cultural capital (Thornton 1995) emerge around them, existing across boundaries of acceptability and

illegality. Effectively these are the locations in which the processes of commodification and marginalisation are being
played out, the carnival performance sites of cultural negotiation. These are acts of performance and meaning-making
and while it has been ably and frequently demonstrated that
the apparently passive act of consuming culture involves the
creation of meaning, such consumption cannot be classed as
performance. Though the acts listed, and the many others
mentioned in this book, are involved in active negotiations
(readings and rewritings), as with mass-produced culture they
all involve the participant in the process of creating their own
performances and artefacts.

As carnival explodes into everyday life so the notion of
closure collapses along with it. As a result the Bakhtinian
notion of a return to law and order and integration can no
longer take place. Victor Turner's notion of reintegration at
the end of any dramatic carnivalesque performance remains
unfinished, leaving the performers of post-modernity socially
suspended and isolated from one another. Instead we are
left with disappointment, dissatisfaction, discontent and the
expectation that the carnival of crime will be performed, must
be performed, again and again (Turner 1983). It is why
Braithewaite's (1989) notion of shaming and reintegration as
a part of the criminal justice system's punishment inventory
simply cannot work outside of anthropological situations, for
there are no longer any events in social life in which such re-
integrative processes could take place. In a sense acts of carnival contain no shame, it is an alien emotion which has no place
either in carnival or the carnival of crime. Without shame the
excitement and carnival of crime run seamlessly through
everyday life with reintegration no longer a possibility.

The carnival of crime

In 1991 and throughout 1992 a number of cities throughout
Britain were thrust into the limelight as sites for joyriding;
not the odd one-off 'TWOCing', but persistent, large-scale
ritualised joyriding. One of these cities was Oxford, although

the 'hotting' itself was very much focused on the Blackbird Leys housing estate just to the south of the city. This was a location that, compared to the rest of Oxford, was not only geographically marginalised, but suffered from a relatively high rate of unemployment, relative poverty and racial heterogeneity. The events that took place here in 1992 were linked to job losses at the nearby Cowley car manufacturing plant. The whole estate existed under the shadow of the car factory; its history and existence were intimately connected with the production and consumption of cars. Cars were both the first and second life of the estate. In the first life they created them and in the second life they celebrated then destroyed them.

As I have pointed out elsewhere:

> The act of joyriding is aptly named, being rich in excitement and a dramatic break from the boredom of being wageless and wealthless in a consumer society. The skills needed to steal a car, which car to steal, how to gain entry, and how to start an engine without a key, all emanate from the culture of male working class life.
>
> (Presdee 1994: 180)

For those on the Blackbird Leys Estate this was particularly true, as their joyriding became a celebration of a particular form of car culture that was carnivalesque in nature, performance centred and criminal. The sport of joyriding went something like this: a team of local youths would spot a hot hatch (the car of choice) and steal it (or arrange with others to have it stolen). It would be delivered to another team who would do it up, delivering it finally to the drivers. In the evenings the cars were raced around the estate, not aimlessly but in a way designed to show off skill. Furthermore, two competing groups (teams) attempted to outdo the other. These displays were watched by certain residents of the estate who, the story goes, were charged a pound for the pleasure, sitting in picnic chairs at the sides of the road. Often after these races the cars were burned on deserted land.

The police were understandably cautious in taking action, since car chases in residential areas are problematic, and although they maintained that the estate was not a 'no-go' area it was difficult territory to control. Furthermore, as the police well knew, a chase only added to the excitement of the circus. Elliot (1992: 22) described how 'the risk of being caught supplies the major thrills, driving along the thin line between arrest and escape'. However, when a local man was seriously injured in a knife attack after he had complained about the hotting, the police, necessarily, moved in with some force. After a period of nightly confrontations the spectacular displays waned.

Blackbird Leys hotting clearly displays elements of classic carnival. First, of course, the event was not for material gain but purely for the pleasure; participants frequently made reference to the thrill and excitement of the displays and any chase that may later have ensued. The pleasure can be seen to derive from two key elements: (1) the proximity of danger, both from the law and from accident or death; and (2) its oppositional status, unashamedly a celebration of doing 'wrong'. It is a challenge to death and to authority, neither being allowed power over the participants. Furthermore there is a symbolic topsy-turvyness involved. The cars used are generally GTIs and other 'hot hatches', expensive and showy, worn as a badge of temporary kingship. Only the best are taken to be abused, finally to be sacrificed in the 'fire', their existence wiped from the world of consumption. It is of course also, whether intentionally or not, an ironic comment on consumption; the image of the car is that of the most desirable in its class, the most expensive and the most protected – the ultimate goal of the car consumer! Its theft, subsequent racing and destruction, with no material gain, subverts its commercial value yet celebrates both its advertised and utility value: providing an exciting drive. But also this act reflects the participants' position in the rational production process. They in a sense repossess the very product they produce but can't afford. They become acquainted once more with their alienated selves – a process that is typical of the carnival. In the ordered world we often cannot possess that which we produce for the affluent, but in the carnival of crime we can. Joyriding is

> an offence to ownership, intellectual or vehicular, being in the end a kind of pure or total gesture of travel, wherein the vehicle, the streets, moving quickly and being out of time and place are enjoyed for themselves, foregrounding the act and skill of driving, not the possession of a car, or the promise of a destruction.
>
> (Hartley 1994: 400)

The reworking of the streets is important, the event contests and, symbolically at least, takes control of a public domain. The performing on the streets of theatre with cars is, at least in part, a celebration of the occupation of the streets in opposition to a municipal ownership, although of course this control is contested between the two rival teams. Most importantly, and this is referred to by those interviewed about the events, the hotting was about identity, demonstrating that one belonged to a group through communal display, thereby constructing an identity of excitement and opposition.

In the end there is no shred of official licence in the Blackbird Leys 'event': its status is in no doubt on either ethical or legislative grounds, it was simply 'illegal', criminal, transgressive. However, one may argue that it occurred because, for those on the estate, there is no other site of carnival, and furthermore the police seem to agree that the spectacle of driving fast is an enjoyable commodity. As a spectacle, statement and act of defiance, it remained unclosed, unresolved, evidence of the daily fragmentation of carnival containing the debris of performed dissent, identified by all as criminal rather than carnival. Yet in reality the experience for the young people of Blackbird Leys concentrated on the carnivalesque rather than the criminal and as such was truly a carnival of crime. This fragmented carnival performance of defiance through driving may now be a more general response to the constraints of time and travel we now live in. As Groombridge (1998b) and Lyng (1998) suggest, we now live in a more generalised 'joyriding culture' where many men and women drivers attempt every day to fulfil their emotional needs through the excitement of driving, hence the emotionality of 'roadrage' and 'joyriding'.

In France it is no surprise that the performance of carnival has also attempted to reclaim the streets. The Friday night and Sunday morning mass inline roller skating on the streets of Paris totally disrupts movement in the city. An average of 30,000 people of all ages embark on a route unknown even to themselves as they twist and turn at great speed through the most congested streets of Paris (see Plate 1). Their sounds of jubilation at the sheer joy of carnival can be heard for miles. Predictably the authorities are close behind as the law is prepared for change and strengthened to criminalise the use of roller blades on the roads. The criminalisation of carnival once more chases the carnival of crime.

Ironically a later exercise in popular carnival, the 'Reclaim the Streets' marches, created the celebration of carnival on major public roads in Britain in order temporarily to close them down as a protest at the amount of traffic on the roads. Later, on 18 June 1999, Reclaim the Streets organised their first carnival against global capitalism in the City of London which contained all the elements of carnival without closure. Later still, on 30 November, they repeated their performance at Euston Station at the same time that 100,000 others plus further hundreds of thousands on the Internet made carnival in full view of the world in Seattle in America to protest at the meeting of the World Trade Organization (known on the Internet as J18 and N30). The authorities once again attempted to close it down. Over one and a half million pounds' worth of policing in London was brought to bear on the carnival, whilst curfews, armoured cars and National Guard units plus violence were used in Seattle.

In the same way that joyriders target 'hot' cars and young people target schools to 'fire', so the carnival against global capitalism targeted the icons of the global economy.

Plate 1 Weekly rollerblade rally through the centre of Paris (Photo by author)

Starbuck's coffee shops and McDonald's restaurants became the targets of carnival excess and through the Internet the Western economy experienced its first major global carnival. This shows that the Internet is not only a site of popular pleasure and transgression but also a truly international site of carnival, with potential to disrupt and disorientate the dominant discourses of global power. The Internet is fast becoming the safe site of the second life of the people. In London the police were beginning to see connections with other carnival performances as they began to see similarities between the carnival on the streets and the underground rave dance culture (*The Times* 1/12/99).

Although the term 'carnival' is rarely used to describe them, social performances such as raves also clearly exhibit these tendencies. Perhaps more closely than any mentioned above, they are ecstatic, of the people, participatory performances. They are excessive, foreground the body and celebrate (or celebrated in the late 1980s) their contraposition to work, indeed the form originated in part as a re-creation of the club culture of Ibiza. The laughter was represented in the most famous symbol of the movement, the smiley face; it was in many ways a most clear example of 'the second life of the people', well some of them anyway. The history of the rise and containment of rave is well discussed and described elsewhere in this book (see chapter 7), illustrating a move by both legislature and mass media to contain and own the phenomenon: the former introducing legislation to outlaw the outdoor and warehouse gatherings; the latter commodifying many of the elements of the event. However, as noted by the likes of Rose (1991) and Thornton (1995), the packaged carnival never tastes as sweet. In this conflict rave clearly illustrated itself as a far deeper cultural performance than the act of going to a disco. At certain points in its history, as now, rave has been contested and it is at these moments that it enters carnival territory.

Both in Bakhtin's carnival and in its (post)-modern equivalents there is a sense in which the participant revolts against the boundaries that keep them 'protected' from life/death.

These boundaries, positioning the performance in the liminal space between the acceptable and the unacceptable, are what makes the activity appealing. The threshold is wide; at one end we have the carnival elements of popular culture such as the licence to humiliate in *Blind Date*; in the middle S&M and rave culture occupy a clearly contested and criminal domain. So what about the far extreme? Does, for example, breaking into schools really contain elements of carnival? Are those very fragments of carnival created by containment?

It was on a weekend that I reversed the process [of truanting] and broke into school with Tony my eldest brother. I was still at the Junior school and he was at the Crypt Grammar, across the green. We went with a friend, on what had been up to then a boring Saturday afternoon. I was surprised that Tony would suggest such a thing, after all he was the eldest and a keen and loyal member of the school scout pack, a choir boy and ought to have known better; but he didn't. I soon learned that I wasn't the only one to be breaking out and breaking in, I had allies. We went that afternoon along the hedge that ran close to the school, easily opening one of the windows to the prefects' dining room. Once inside, we closed the frosted window quietly and slowly edged our way to the door, Tony slowly turning the handle and easing the door open just a crack. Instantly, through the crack, noise thundered in, pushing back our bravado and stopping our breath. We experienced the immediate high of adrenaline mixed with fear, that surged through our bodies and made me feel faint. There was somebody else in the building! The caretaker, the headmaster, police? We didn't know. Tony pushed the door again, whilst I looked backwards thinking of escape routes and going through my repertoire of stories and explanations that I might need. Tony began to laugh.

'Hello Bry.' He giggled.

'Hello Tone.'

I glimpsed over his shoulder and there, down the corridor, keeping low below the windows were other boys going up and down the stairs and running in and out of the classrooms. To my relief it seemed that half the estate was there and it turned out it was a favourite Saturday afternoon playground. They couldn't keep them in on weekdays; they couldn't keep them out on weekends!

(Presdee 1988)

4 Commodification, consumption and crime

In the post-modern world of 'consuming passions' (Williamson 1988) there are a number of dynamics that are rightly the concern of cultural criminology. First there is the process of the commodification of everyday life, including crime and violence. Second there is the absolute necessity for the legal or illegal consumption of commodities for the reproduction of both the economic system and our social 'selves'. Commodities themselves appear, as Marx (1977: 435) commented, 'a very trivial thing and easily understood . . . it is in reality a very queer thing, abounding in metaphysical subtleties and theological niceties'. However the relationship between the production and commodification process, and the distribution and consumption process, takes on a supreme significance in late modernity.

> In a culture in which the supreme goal is to have . . . and to have more and more . . . and in which one can speak of someone as 'being worth a million dollars', how can there be an alternative between having and being? On the contrary, it would seem that the very essence of being is having; that if one has nothing, one is nothing.
>
> (Fromm 1976: 3)

It is worth quoting Erich Fromm further on contemporary capitalism as he unravels the connections between violent acts, crime and consumption.

It means: that I want everything for myself; that possessing, not sharing, gives me pleasure; that I must become
greedy because if my aim is having, I am more the more I
have; that I must feel antagonistic toward all others: my
customers whom I want to deceive, my competitors
whom I want to destroy, my workers whom I want to
exploit. I can never be satisfied because there is no end to
my wishes; I must be envious of those who have more and
afraid of those who have less. But I have to repress all
these feelings in order to represent myself as the smiling,
rational, sincere, kind human being everybody pretends
to be . . . Greed and peace preclude each other.

(Fromm 1976: xxviii)

Here individualism, greed, destruction, dishonesty, fear and
violence are woven, through the processes of production and
consumption, inevitably into all our everyday lives. Now
crime, in the form of a commodity, enables us all to consume
without cost as we enjoy the excitement, and the emotions of
hate, rage and love that crime often contains.

Strange events happen to us all as we meander through the
marketplaces of modernity; events that become so commonplace that we pay little or no attention to them. For example,
some time ago violence, crime and excitement intruded into
my ordinary peaceful Saturday shopping expedition just
when I least expected it, in what was normally a quiet corner
of an electrical goods shop in the middle of Canterbury.
There, surrounded by walls of televisions, a small crowd of
people had gathered, heads at an angle, buried in the action
coming from the mega-screen set above them. They were
oblivious to where they were, insulated and isolated from
each other as they individually and eagerly consumed the
noise, thrills and excitement that was placed in front of them.
A young women shop assistant darted back and forth across
the shop, pulling in new customers and consumers into the
excitement of the moment. From the television monitor came
the noise and frenzied voices of the carnival of the chase –
a police chase, but more importantly a *real* police chase

complete with swerves, skids, crashes and victims. They were consuming in a blissful state of 'non-responsibility' the top-rated video *Police Stop*, comprising a complete video of police helicopter 'footage' of real car chases that 'begins with a bang'. The blurb on the box states, 'no actors, no stunt men, no script, this is real life action as it happens captured on camera by the police'. The young assistant spoke feverishly to me, 'It's great! It's great! It starts with a big crash. It's all real! It's all real!', her face flushed with excitement. 'It's great, it's better than the films. At least you know it really happened!' A number of questions come to mind here (not least of which is how the police could possibly become involved in the production and creation of crime and excitement as a commodity to be sold and consumed through the entertainment market), including how the commodification process is affecting everyday life experiences and behaviour. Here we have an example of the power of capitalism to extend its processes of production, distribution and consumption to include emotions and actions especially in the realm of cultural creation which becomes dominated by commodification. In this case it is the commodification of the excitement of crime alongside human emotions and values. Crime and violence have become objectified and commodified and, as such, much desired whilst being distributed through various forms of media to be pleasurably consumed.

As Slater (1997: 27) has argued,

> All social relations, activities and objects can in principle be exchanged as commodities. This is one of the most profound secularizations enacted by the modern world. Everything can become a commodity at least during some part of its life. This potential for anything, activity or experience, to be commodified or to be replaced by commodities perpetually places the intimate world of the everyday into the impersonal world of the market and its values. Moreover, while consumer culture appears universal because it is depicted as a land of freedom in which everyone can be a consumer, it is also felt to be universal

because everyone must be: this particular freedom is compulsory.

The development of the all-consuming individual, driven by emotions, runs alongside the development of the commodification of more and more aspects of our lives, where education has become a commodity, health a commodity, love and religion a commodity. Introduction columns now take large spaces in local and national newspapers, whilst the simple act of talking to strangers, what Simmel termed 'sociability' (the one act he thought would fall outside of the commodification process [Frisby 1992: 132]), has peculiarly become an enjoyable consumer item for young people and a lucrative market for chat lines. Groups of clergy now meet to manage the souls of their multi-church parishes and to decide the most efficient and effective way to deliver the commodity of spiritual guidance to their clients. Indeed, young people are becoming attracted to the rave-like mass warehouses of a range of modern churches where what is important, as in all consumption, is the immediacy of the experience and the obsolescence of the commodity (Lefebvre 1971: 81).

Obsolescence becomes an important part of everyday life as our lives become characterised by the sell-by date of commodities. We need to savour the consumption process and check if we have the shelf-life left to do it. In the end we desire obsolescence, it becomes a need and is dutifully built into commodities. All must be transitory: emotions, relationships, things. We are judged not by what we own but by our ability to consume, to use, to finish up completely, in the old sense of consumption. Without consumption there can be no social life and no social identity. When identity comes not from production but consumption, then in the same way that many who did not produce were in some way parted from the central processes of society, so many who do not have the ability to consume are only provided with this ability through the processes of social policy. So in the same way that it is necessary for production to be organised, so it becomes necessary for consumption to be organised and for all to be in some way included, or in 'third way' terms, 'integrated'. In the midst of this we become a 'wanting' society where we strive to give to all some form of affluence that results in 'wanting' forever, therefore inevitably weaving us into the exploitation of work where we labour to reproduce our daily desires. At the same time the consumption process continually enlarges our appetites so that we can never be full and 'desire', as Lefebvre (1971: 118) points out, 'can neither be extinguished nor grasped, its very essence is unknown; for it is elusive and when defined as instinctive or sexual . . . it breaks out in the form of cruelty, madness, violence, the unpredictable.'

Simmel, as Frisby has shown, 'was aware . . . of the extension of commodification and of the commodification of leisure and human experience as well' (Frisby 1992: 170) and went on to suggest that there was a 'craving today for excitement' without 'thinking it important for us to find out why these stimulate us' (Simmel 1990). He thereby highlighted the flight from reality that is reflected in the process of distancing oneself from the strictures of rationality and objectivity and the 'removal of deeper content' in life in contrast to the 'dreadful, shocking, tragic nature of modern life' (Simmel 1990). Once more the blissful state of the 'non-responsibility' of consumption blankets our ability to be interested in the processes of production and the exploitation and cruelty that may be involved. This rests of course on the individualism and isolation of consumption, for to consume is the ultimate solitary act of a society of 'isolated millions' who lack the ability to communicate other than through the mediation of another commodity, namely the commodity of entertainment and the media.

The efficiency at any price that modern economic forms demand produces a culture that both recognises the demands of consumption and produces meanings of its own. Against an increasingly individualised and secularised everyday life stand the dominant structures of State and Market, with the State continuing to bureaucratise everyday life in contest with the Market, which strives to commodify it. In this struggle the Market has proved to be the dominant force in the inner dynamics of late modernity whereby bureaucracy itself has succumbed to the pressures of the Market and become a commodity in itself. It is at this point that we begin to create a culture where the process of the consumption of commodities itself generates the meanings and motivations for life that creates an identity that is both individualistic yet is celebrated en masse.

Unlike the rhythms of production – clocking on/clocking off, time off/time on – there can be no such rhythm to consumption. Time conforms to the necessities of the social system, not the experienced necessities of living. The time sense acquired from working under capitalism comes to condition life activities in general. The work sense of time usurps that of life. Production is rational; pleasure is irrational. Consumption as pleasure becomes both an irrational act and the 'filling in of time and consciousness' in the 'social spaces of distraction and display'. We must consume not one day a week but continually. We demand more and more products that become more and more 'dematerialised' (Slater 1997) and meaningless: 'signs without significance'.

As everyday life becomes less and less interesting, so it also becomes less and less bearable and there is felt a general desire for daily excitement that becomes an essential ingredient in a consumer commodity culture. Excitement is now created for consumption in a multitude of manners such as bungee jumping, spectacular rides, ballooning, theme parks and carnivals, all aimed at the commodification of excitement. All these need to be bought at the market rate. The experience of excitement can also be attained by a large range of criminal activities. Bank fraud and theft, joyriding, manipulating the stock market, all contain the thrills and spills of edge-work. In a society that demands excitement and desire in order to keep the momentum of the marketplace, we can expect the problems associated with the quest for excitement to become both enduring and extensive. The general 'collective' yearn is now for spectacle and experience as we become consumers of imagery. As such we have lost our capacity for astonishment, wonder and curiosity in a world that no longer moves us in an emotional way. There is a high fantasy factor within emotional life and existence that creates the need for immediate satisfaction which in turn becomes the driving force of violence. In this world the desire for excitement can, for some, only be satisfied through senseless acts of violence and destruction. In this way the images we consume become devoid of context and become infantile and immediate. As Schopenhauer points out, this outlook is like 'the childish delusion that books, like eggs, must be enjoyed when they are fresh' (Schopenhauer 1969: 1470).

In this world based on sensations and emotions the individual is revered and nurtured. It is a Disney-like world based on the immediacy of and need for fun and pleasure. In everyday life and education in particular, there is an emphasis on morale rather than morality. Here institutions strive to achieve activity without pain. Learning must be fun; poverty must be fun; housework must be fun; and as in *Clockwork Orange* and even *Wind in the Willows* (where Toad steals a car and partakes in what must be the first literary joyride) violence, crime and disorder must be fun.

There is here a strange tension between the rationality (organisation) demanded by production and consumption and the irrationality of senseless consumption needed to reproduce the cycle. As science and rational liberalism attempt to order everyday life and meaning-making, so irrationality is banished to the act of consumption, as irrational acts themselves become commodified, acting as a bridge to the displaced world of the upside down. It is part of the 'consuming of displays, displays of consuming, consuming of displays of consuming, consuming of signs and signs of consuming' (Lefebvre 1971: 108). The endless, senseless and irrational appears a necessary ingredient of contemporary life as we strive through consumption to push back the ordering of rationality and return once more to the comfort of anarchy, disorder and irrationality. Violence itself is not to do with a rational approach to life but is connected to the personal gratification gleaned from the excitement of the superiority of 'winning'. The consumption of crime becomes a blissful state of 'non-responsibility', a sort of never-ending 'moral holiday' where we can enjoy in private immoral acts and emotions.

The move from the irrational to the rational and the yearning for the spectacle of spontaneity were identified by Weber when he described the task of the 'spirit' of capitalism as the 'destruction of spontaneous impulsive enjoyment' (Weber 1978: 119), which would herald the rise of civilisation and the displacement of the irrational by the rational. Freud outlined a need for stimulation, balanced by the need to reduce the level of tension, thanatos, the death instinct. Simmel examined conflict and co-operation and the resultant war–peace rhythm and went on, in the 'Sociology of Space' (Simmel 1903), to connect the notion of impulsiveness and freedom to the process of escaping the new constraints and regulations of a system of production that relied heavily on uniformity and rationality. The development of a system of scientific 'time' as a form of regulation within systems of production brought even heavier constraints to the spirit of spontaneity, creating the second-by-second regulation of everyday life. Resisting time thus became an important element of deviance, dissent and carnival.

If then the process of production increasingly creates structures of constraint, then the burden of everyday life itself becomes more and more unbearable, leading as Fromm suggested to the 'compulsion to escape unbearable situations' (Fromm 1960: 133). The 'thwarting of the whole of man's sensuous, emotional and intellectual capacities' he saw as related to acts of destruction and violence and their enjoyment. He went on to say that 'the amount of destructiveness to be found in individuals is proportionate to the amount to which the expansiveness of life is curtailed' (Fromm 1960: 138). Here it is social conditions that are important; they lead to the 'suppression of life' which produces the 'passion for destruction'. This is the suppression that Weber saw as the tendency in modern life to 'uniformity in styles of life which is nowadays supported by the capital interests in the standardisation of production' (Weber 1948: 78).

Consumption of the irrational remains an important connecting bridge to pre-productive life. Here the marketplace and the process of consumption take on an extraordinarily important role in the creation of self and identity. Now in the ever-expanding realm of commodification and consumption, acts of hurt and humiliation, death and destruction, all become inextricably woven into processes of pleasure, fun and performance. We all participate in the creation of crime as we consume the filming of the carnival of the chase, becoming part of the process of production of real crime and real violence. It is not just the criminals but also the police, the public and the media who all play a part. If young people don't steal cars there can be no chase. If the police don't chase there is no event. If the event is not filmed there can be no product. If the product is not communicated there can be no distribution. If we don't watch there is no consumption and the process of production distribution and consumption is incomplete. So when we do watch, we consume and become willing partners in the creation of crime itself and willing consumers of the excitement it produces.

In its consumption, violence is simplified and reduced to a trivial act of instant enjoyment; it thereby becomes no different from, say, the eating of a chocolate biscuit or the drinking of a can of coke. There is no moral debate, no constraint, no remorse, no meaning. This is disposable violence that need not concern us or delay us in our journey through the week. It is violence without responsibility. No John Pilger to debate it, no *Panorama* programme to attack our sensitivities. Just simple, real violence that we can all enjoy; crime that we can all enjoy; humiliation that we can all enjoy. The production, distribution and consumption process itself masks the oppressive relationships between the powerful and the powerless involved in the process, concentrating as it does on the fulfilment of desires and the satiation of emotions. For example, in the production of pornography, women in particular are humiliated during the actual making of the product itself. In the consumption of pornography women in general are humiliated but the processes of production are hidden within the processes of desire and pleasure.

The question then arises as to whether the producers of crime and violence commodities are actively involved in creating a *need* for the consumption of their cruel commodities, in the same way that producers of all products create new needs every day. That is, will there be pressure on producers to create new forms of their product that would be a 'new and improved' violence? Or violence in a disposable 'family pack' for family consumption, when it will become an everyday enjoyable experience and a 'fact' of life?

> Somewhere, sometime, I started to steal; from my father, the paper shop, the church collection, Woolworths, Ron next door. Suddenly, it seemed, I was aware of 'wanting' and of being 'without' as advertising and consumerism, driven by the new postwar wealth, began to be part of my life. When I was very young you either had or you didn't; not really conscious of needing possessions, but simply 'having' or 'not having', yet needing to 'have', to be 'part of'. To join in. I wanted to possess: to be a consumer, to own, to escape into the world of the object. Possessing was visual; everyone could see what you were, what you owned: toys, clothes, school uniform, sports gear, food, even haircuts. Our lives were made up of 'show and tell'. Mum used to cut our hair herself, a skill she said she had been trained for. All I knew was that the hair was shaved off short, with no style, presenting the whole world with a sixty foot sign that said 'home-made'. The same sort of messages that home-made clothes give out even though the pattern cover says 'Paris design' or 'Vogue original', usually it all ended up looking 'home-made'. When I was in my teens I had to be taken, struggling, to the executioner's chair for this regular hair operation, and I would cry tears of rage and hate, knowing that I would be laughed at until it began to 'grow out'.
>
> (Presdee 1988)

Part II

Context

5 Hurt, humiliation and crime as popular pleasure

I was horrified several years ago at my own emotional re-
actions to a world championship boxing match that ended in
dramatic scenes of death and dying. I realised then that what I
had been enjoying were two men systematically, and legally,
beating each other to death. If indeed I had recorded the fight,
as no doubt millions did, I would now be in possession of my
own 'snuff' movie, to replay at my own convenience and for
my continual enjoyment whenever I felt the need. The question I asked myself was how had I come to be sucked in by the
razzmatazz and hype of the promoters, so that I would sit
down with a drink by my side and get excited by watching a
man being beaten to death.

This was real violence, manufactured for enjoyment
through a sophisticated and commercially organised global
industry specifically for consumption through a global media.
Unlike Shakespeare's *Macbeth* or the film *Pulp Fiction*, the
actors wouldn't get up after the curtain came down and go to
the pub and retell stories of yet another great performance;
this was real death and real violence without the constraints
and framework of theatre. And so it is with more general
television programmes such as Cilla Black's *Blind Date*,
where young people are persuaded to divulge to the viewing
public the innermost secrets of their 'partner for the week'.
Not acted out but in 'real life'. What are their weaknesses,
how can we laugh at them and strip them of their dignity?
Embarrassment and humiliation are the name of the game

and participants play it with a vengeance to the enjoyment of the crowd and the viewing 'public'. Of course the participants sign a confidentiality document that restricts them from telling how the programme was made, thereby keeping hidden the processes of the production of humiliation. Often they are no match for the media experts who contort and control their emotions for the sake of the ratings, and as a result monetary profit. This then is part of the process of the commodification of all aspects of our lives that has been such a feature of contemporary society during the last ten years. Now violence, crime, humiliation and cruelty are being created especially for consumption through the various sound, print and visual media outlets of television, radio, video and the Internet. They are no longer simply the result of social relationships and structural configurations. Now violence, crime, humiliation and cruelty are also part of the processes of production and display all the characteristics of such a process.

The product becomes alienated from the process so that images of people dying in weather disasters, when seen in entertainment-style weather programmes, are about the inevitability of death and the excitement of observing it rather than as images that say something about tragedy and trauma. Media mogul Chris Evans has the ability to reduce people to tears on radio and still be immensely popular. Jeremy Beadle and other home video show producers can attract ratings because we hope to see misfortune as it happens. The TV programme *Gladiators* inspired young women to attack each other with weapons and then discuss the battle in detail afterwards and still be cheered on by young and old alike. Reality media is with us and humiliation television has arrived, whilst cruelty in many forms has become a commodity that needs to be produced day after day specifically for our consumption.

Like all raw materials these emotions and actions occur 'naturally' but are finite. When stocks become difficult to attain, they are manufactured, processed and produced by the media industry, then packaged, distributed and finally consumed. The search for 'naturally' occurring suffering, violence and crime is a continuing exploration process for the media industry. This is why the discovery of new famines, weather disasters (often wrongly labelled natural disasters) and wars are followed by them closely and even hunted down by the global media. Documentaries such as Carlton Television's *Savage Seas* describes itself as being about 'beauty' and 'violence'; that is, the aesthetics of violence. Whilst Katherine Flett, television journalist for the *Observer* newspaper, in describing the content of the BBC's *Twister Week* natural disaster programme went on to say:

> There were poignant interviews with bath tub survivors. Debbie LaFrance from Texas found herself in a tree when God lost his patience playing a game of Happy Families and blew her home away. . . . Her daughter survived but what was left of her husband ended up several blocks down the road.
>
> (*Observer* 4/7/99)

What the viewer was watching was the point of death as entertainment, unlike Robert Capa's famous image of a soldier as he is killed in the Spanish Civil War which he hoped would make us think about war. Now we can experience the pain of privations, the suffering of war, the real fear of violence and crime, all in the privacy of our own homes. How we experience it the producer cares little about. Whether we are thrilled by it, shocked by it, turned on by it or horrified by it is of no concern to the manufacturer.

Nevertheless, how we are affected by it and how we respond to it are of increasing concern to media regulators, as more and more producers are being held to account for the responses of the audience. In May 1999 a jury in Michigan came close to a verdict of 'death by television' when they found the producers of the *Jenny Jones* show to be responsible for the killing of a guest, Scott Amedure, shot by another guest, Jonathan Schmitz, who discovered on the show, in front of a live audience, that Scott was a secret sexual admirer. The jury awarded the family of the murdered man $25 million.

Robert Lichter of the Centre for Media and Public Affairs in Washington was reported as saying 'Talk shows play on the public humiliation of emotionally vulnerable people' (*The Times* 14/5/99).

The never-ending process of commodification under contemporary capitalism dovetails neatly with the increasing need for privately enjoyed, carnivalesque transgression. As the 'official' world of politics, rationality and science tracks down transgression, so the 'second life' of the people erupts as private pleasure. Dog-fighting remains as popular as fox-hunting only hidden, except of course on the modern site of carnival the Internet. Bare-knuckle fighting continues to be popular in practice, although the David Monaghan documentary *Bare Fist* was recently refused a viewing certificate whilst in a fight near Düsseldorf men dressed in barbed wire beat each other with baseball bats (*London Evening Standard* 24/11/99) and American Doug Dedge died in a fight in Kiev in the Ukraine which was billed as 'a fight without rules' (*Independent* 20/3/98). Unofficial car racing and rallies manage still to be both popular and survive, and there are even reports of cock-fighting still being organised in parts of England. Over the last 25 years the RSPCA has prosecuted a number of people for 'quail' fighting, with over 100 people involved in one contest alone. In 1997 there were 17 arrests at a cock-fight on Bexley Heath and in 1992 there were 12 arrests at a Potters Bar dog-fight. In November 1999 there was a mass killing of 15 badgers in one set in Essex (*Times* 4/11/99) and earlier three men were caught badger-baiting near the northern city of Durham and were sentenced to five months in gaol. The stipendiary magistrate Ian Gillespie, in defining their pleasures as criminal, commented: 'Civilised society will not countenance such violent behaviour which you no doubt regard as sport.' (We are left to wonder if he would have defined fox-hunting in the same way.) The RSPCA continues to receive reports of badger-baiting, of dogs fighting men and dogs fighting monkeys. All this in spite of 'fighting' animals being officially banned since 1835. These events have reportedly taken place in such places as barns, gamekeepers' lodges, house cellars and even in one case a school swimming pool.

Whereas the early carnival constituted community, so the fragmentation of carnival festers in the realm of private pleasures provided most often by the modern media. This never-ending process of commodification demands the never-ending consumption of 'reality' entertainment that contains real violence, real crime and real humiliation. This is not ironic violence but real violence, real humiliation and real hurt. It is here in reality television that we become acquainted with birth, the body and death rather than from the public performances of carnival as in the past. Now in the seclusion and privacy of our own homes we can join in with the illicit and the grotesque as we consume humiliation shows, watch real death and destruction and converse daily through the Internet with others who share our felt oppression, our hates, our excitement or our revulsion. This fragmented second life, experienced in private, is our own personal site of wrong-doing as we transgress without remorse, without punishment and without sanction. For example, Andrew Sullivan of the *Sunday Times* described *The Jerry Springer Show* as 'postmodern violent fantasy' and went on say that what we as viewers experience was a 'deeply guilty pleasure . . . the compulsive enjoyment of something you are completely appalled by' (*Sunday Times* 17/10/99).

Reality entertainment comes in many forms. There is the television of the 'catastrophe', where everyday death is the commodity (e.g. *Fire Rescue 999*); sporting violence videos that rarely fall outside the top ten video list such as *Trouble on the Terraces* or *Tyson Uncaged* ('He's mad, he's bad and he's back!'); car crashes and *Crime Watch* style programmes that continue to pull in the ratings with video titles such as *Car Wars* ('The all-time greatest smashes and crashes') or *Bike Wars*. There is a continuing endeavour to create more palatable and entertaining forms of violence and humiliation such as elements of *Gladiators* (now out of production in the UK), *Blind Date* (see the Broadcasting Standards 1996 report) or the more recent *Something for the Weekend* with its game-show format based on sexual humiliation.

Not only can we consume it but we can also produce it. In a Sontagian sense, with the onset of camcorder technology, we are faced with the dilemma of whether to intervene in social acts or to film them. Do we prevent accidents or do we film them and send them to Jeremy Beadle or other camcorder shows, and allow the whole country to enjoy the 'spectacle'? In this world the desire for excitement can only be satisfied through irrational acts where content and context become secondary to immediate experience. Along with this world based on fun and pleasure the motivation for action becomes predicated on the fulfilling of desire and pleasure without the pain of effort. Now, as learning must be fun, so too poverty must be fun, violence fun, humiliation fun, degradation fun.

As Katz (1988) has pointed out, there appears to be a seduction as we run along the edge of 'shame'. Watching young people divulge to us the innermost secrets of their 'partner for a week' in *Blind Date* and become part of a public act of humiliation for our own pleasure allows us to stand outside the moral code and collectively to break it. It allows us to play at being deviant, at being collectively evil, and to share a collective thrill that stands outside of reality. The more real the experience, the more real the thrill, and the more we can be like a real evil person. The enactment of real drama and real crime blurs the boundaries between fact and fiction. We consider such dramas to be more real than fiction, indeed to be real. We can take part in real-life drama and in some sense we can 'be there'. Rather than reality television being on the extremes of law and order and public condemnation, it can also be understood as approval of the act we are watching. We can join in, enjoy it, be seduced by it. Reality television is in a sense how we all privately transgress. It is a chance to see how 'it', that is crime, is done, not how we think it's done, and to enjoy doing wrong from the safety of our own homes. We can be criminal in reality rather than fiction.

At the same time we seek to share our everyday lives and all our vulnerabilities and weaknesses with whoever offers us confidentiality and sociability. Our fears and weaknesses, our dislikes and desires can all be used against us in this rational, scientific society and therefore we seek to 'talk' our transgressions to the third person, the outsider. The 'barmaid' and the 'barman' were the traditional cultural icons of the third person standing outside of reality. The third person, the clown or the jester, stood traditionally 'outside' of the constraints of society and in that way was protected from the sanctions of society for his or her transgressions. We have a social need to talk to the 'unconnected', the 'uninvolved', a non-person who appears to relate yet not judge.

A friend who was dying told me that people who weren't particularly close friends kept visiting him and telling him all their problems, talking of their failing marriages, careers, and feelings of desperation as well as their transgressions and their wrong-doings, all things they had never shared before. They were, he told me, sharing for the first time their lives with someone who had no investment in life, who would take all their secrets with him. They believed that their transgressions would die with him. As well as being the 'confidant', the third person also mocks and outrages authority, is grotesque and breaks the rules, transgresses for us all. The modern media pretend to be the third brave person of modernity. But in reality we are betrayed as our individual lives and deeply personal identities are commodified and consumed by others. The modern media don't mock *for* us, they mock *at* us. They don't become an 'ass' – they make an 'ass' out of us and in no way do they represent the modern '*flâneur*' of Walter Benjamin. The mass of society bare their souls to the media who, in turn, transform them into the commodity of entertainment. Confidentialities are turned against the subject, transforming them into the object of hurt and humiliation as their social being is commodified ready for consumption.

At the same time commodity fetishism enables consumption to reach a sublime state of 'non-responsibility', where the commodity, ripped from history, appears magically conceived, coming from nowhere and produced by no one. Its consumption affects no one, dispossesses no one, exploits no one. In *Gladiators* young women athletes, who were once champions of field or track, earned a living by 'hitting' other women. Hitting people becomes like all consumption, which seeks to hide the production process and the alienation that is created. No moral debate, no constraints, no remorse, no meaning. Disposable violence produced in a disposable pack. In this sense acts of violence are perceived of in a different way, responded to in a different way. But, importantly, they are created specially for us, they are truly a commodity, standing outside of vicarious experience. Unlike drama this is the creation of real events of violence, humiliation or cruelty to be experienced in a different way to theatre. Raymond Williams' (1974) notion of the 'dramatised society', where he argued that the density of drama through modern media has brought a sense of the 'dramatic' to everyday life, needs now to be developed further to understand that the vicarious, the dramatic, has given way to multiple realities. We make sense of life not through drama but through the realities of all. We don't explore humiliation through drama, rather we experience it through someone's lived reality. We don't intellectualise it, we watch it and transpose ourselves into it. We don't want to think it but feel it. We don't want it filtered through culture but as unadorned, uncontaminated, immediate experience. When Docker (1996: 281) suggests that '[p]opular commercial television offers its collective drama as a sprawl of composite "life": as the permanent mixed eruption of excitement, spectacle, happiness, joy, tragedy, sadness, loss, conflict, dilemma, terror, horror and death', then we can apply all of this 'sprawl' to existing reality television programmes. Early morning chat shows act out 'real' moral or social dilemmas, confronting often unsuspecting members of the audience with the dilemmas of their lives. Did you know your husband/wife/partner was having an affair with the person in the front row? Did you know that your daughter/son took drugs? Hated you? Was having an affair with your sister/ brother/next door neighbour? Other programmes confront the audience with a particular tragedy as it unfolds. Video programmes share mainly accidents with us so we can enjoy the hurt of others. And so all the 'sprawl' that Docker talks of as being provided by drama, the 'vicarious televisual cheap-thrill' described by Fenwick and Hayward (2000) is no longer in the forefront of the creation of consciousness. Drama cannot bring the 'immediacy' that modern consumption demands because it is a form of reality refracted through culture; it provides a vicarious experience that contains within it elements of reality but is not and cannot be reality. The 'natural' development of the media, initially through the print medium then television and sound, is to provide for a seamless experience whereby the immediacy of the experience of consumption continues into the immediacy of the experiences of reality television. We are not being prepared to consume, we simply continue to consume. Now we gain all we know about our 'world' direct from experience rather than thought.

Immediacy and spectacle come together in the media schedules. As David Harvey pointed out:

> The image, the appearance, the spectacle can all be experienced with an intensity (joy or terror) made possible by their appreciation as pure and unrelated presents in time. . . . The immediacy of events, the sensationalism of the spectacle (political, scientific, military, as well as those of entertainment), become the stuff of which consciousness is forged.
>
> (Harvey 1989: 54)

The struggle for 'spectacle' has given rise within the media to the spectacle of the creation of spectacle. In July 1999 the BBC *Everyman* programme attempted to make a sensational story concerning 'sex addicts'. Unknown to them, a female reporter from the *Sun* newspaper posed as a 'sex addict', thus creating a further spectacular story for the *Sun*. The BBC response was to sue the *Sun* for spoiling their spectacle. The BBC was further involved in the problems of creating a spectacular product when their *Inside Story* team became inextricably linked in the unfolding life history of Arez

Tivoni. Tivoni, who claimed to be suffering from amnesia, was flown by the *Inside Story* team to Israel to trace his children in order for the spectacle to be filmed. Unbeknown to the programme makers, the father had a history of violence and when he found his children at a battered wives refuge where his wife was staying for her own protection, he killed them. In this way the *Inside Story* team unwittingly became involved in the killing of children and were as much a part of the history of that event as the family itself. They were in the business of the creation of spectacle for consumption following the very trends I have described above. Ros Coward of the *Guardian* newspaper commented after this particular event: 'Even serious programmes are following a tabloid agenda where researchers pounce on extreme situations that promise a good story. . . . If the subjects are extreme, so much the better' (*Guardian* 6/7/99).

The ultimate making of personal history as spectacle came in January 1999 with the marrying of two strangers, chosen through a competition, by Birmingham radio station BRMB. This mirrored a similar event that had taken place in Sydney the year before. In both cases the couples separated later but something that was now an important part of their lives and personal social and sexual histories was long forgotten by the media. Reality had been both created and consumed. And in America the special programme *Who Wants to Marry a Millionaire?* rated 20 million viewers who watched alleged millionaire Rick Rockwell pick a wife from a list of 50 women. Later it was found that he had a restraining order placed against him for acting violently to a former fiancee. The final act in making relationships came on radio Key 103 in Britain, when a couple won a divorce for wanting it more than any other couple.

Closely connected to spectacle is the notion of humiliation and the forces of public degradation. To be humiliated is to become objectified and propelled by forces outside of our control, where we literally lose control over our identities as we are driven down by all manner of degrading, debasing and deflating attacks. In such cases our identity and personal worth are mugged in a violent power struggle where those with authority and power humiliate those without. Television thus provides for us the spectacle of humiliation as entertainment. Is the fun we get out of it because we are pleased it isn't us? Or is it more our response to the immersion into a collective evilness, where the more real the experience, the more real the thrill, heightened by the knowledge that our excitement at watching humiliation will go undetected by the forces of law and order? In Britain there is *Vanessa* (now discontinued) and *Kilroy* and *Esther* of the BBC and *Tricia* of ITV. In the United States humiliation chat shows abound with Jerry Springer, Ricki Lake and Jenny Jones leading the way. One of the latest more unashamed, upfront humiliation programmes was presented by Ulrika Johnson in August 1999 entitled *Mother Knows Best* which was described by the *Guardian*'s Michele Hanson in the following way: 'There sits the son, hunched, embarrassed, inarticulate, but still smiling at his mother, a hag who humiliates him as we watch' (*Guardian* 13/8/99). But of course it is soon the mother's turn to be publicly humiliated as the stereotypical interfering woman who ruins our lives and deserves such treatment. Hanson continues, 'It isn't a celebration, it's a set up, worse than Jerry Springer. At least his programmes humiliate everyone in the family'.

The programme *Change of Heart* has a failsafe double humiliation formula whereby already dating couples choose another 'blind date' against which to measure their existing partner. The climax is whether they choose the old or new partner and enables both to be humiliated publicly. For the viewer there is guaranteed public humiliation as the choice is made. As Hoff of the *Guardian* writes with this particular programme in mind, 'Television is not where we turn for veracity, but for entertainment and . . . watching couples hash up their relationships with selfish "trial dating" is probably wrong, but surprisingly compelling' (*Guardian* 29/6/99). Here the truth of transgressive pleasure is made clear. There is something seductive about enjoying something we ought not to be enjoying and the thrill of the transgression is heightened by the 'reality' factor. Watching an actor humiliating another in a 'soap opera' is one thing, but watching real people being really humiliated for our entertainment is another, and involves a different order of emotions, pleasures and desires.

Another version of an existing American programme *Cheaters* is soon to be made. It is based on unfaithful spouses being secretly filmed through keyholes by their furious partners who then leap into action and start pulling hair, which again demonstrates the current appetite for real-life entertainment. Meanwhile, the Denise Van Outen show *Something for the Weekend* had a segment where a young woman identified her fiancé by studying a line-up of male genitalia. The *Sunday Times*, reflecting on this thirst for humiliation, commented that 'to a sizeable section of the public the random humiliation' involved was 'preferable to that doled out by Jeremy Paxman on *Newsnight* on BBC2' (*Sunday Times* 17/10/99). And in the summer of the year 2000 much of Britain seemed to openly enjoy collectively humiliating the 'inmates' of Channel 4's *Big Brother* house, who subjected themselves to national humiliation and psychosocial dissection while endeavouring to win a prize of £70,000.

The print media have always been leaders in providing consumers with transgressive pleasures. Comic strips and 'Penny dreadfuls' have a long history of connecting the bizarre, sex and violence together in a fictional way, whereas contemporary magazines have, like television, moved from fiction to fact; from fantasy to reality. The magazine *Bizarre* (subtitled 'More Balls less Bollocks', which illustrates its claim to be a 'laddish' publication) has a circulation of over 100,000 plus a readership of half a million and is readily available at a newsagent near you as well as at W.H. Smiths. This is a prime example of a carnivalesque publication that portrays a world upside down, where pleasure is to do with suffering, sex and violence, and where laughter is at the heart of irrationality. *Bizarre* is a contemporary cultural artefact that portrays our everyday fascination with the extreme, with the emphasis always on fun and enjoyment. It celebrates and concentrates openly on the irrational, the unacceptable, the inhuman of our 'second life' but more than anything on the real. Its stories have included features on dog-fighting (Jan. '99) and backstreet brawlers (Jan. '99), where Jon Hotten talks about unlicensed boxing and describes a real fight rather than a fight controlled by rules and regulations: 'Pro-fights have a sheen of unreality. Here the sensation is barer. The punches sounded like punches complete with the suckings of breath and the snorts of pain and surprise as they landed' (*Bizarre* Jan. '99: 39). Other stories talk of the 'Art of the nasty' (Feb. '99), 'Black Xmas: disaster, murder and mayhem' (Jan. '99), with other features instructing the reader on 'drawing your own blood' or 'drinking liquid nitrogen'. The 'special sealed section' of May 1999 contained a full-page illustration of the 'death' photographs of Nazi war criminals hung at Nuremberg. The 'special section' of August 1999 contained the 'top ten weirdest porn mags ever', which clearly shows the intent to make sexual gratification a central aim of the publication. The overall theme of sex, death and violence is reflected in its adverts, such as the one for the Lady Ninja video subtitled 'The extremist all-girl Ninja sex and violence action movie series' or those for CDs such as 'Sex and the Dead' as well as the CapCom adverts for martial arts swords ('Knock em dead') and axes ('sure to be this season's must-have weapon').

Bizarre contains within it many of the characteristics of carnival – 'repugnance yet fascination; power, desire, and disorder; where all, irrespective of wealth or morality, join in a world upside-down' (Presdee 1994: 182) – as well as the commodification of crime and violence for consumption as illegal and irrational pleasure. Its section on 'The Worst of the Web' takes its readers into the contemporary site of transgressive pleasures *par excellence* and the realm of reality entertainment that other forms of media such as television are attempting to follow. Michael Christian of Websidestory, a company that ranks Internet traffic, commented:

Wherever the adult business goes the rest of the net follows . . . large non-sexual operators like amazon.com are

Plate 2a Club-Dead homepage, January 2000

"Last year I took a trip to Paris and toured the Musee d'Orsay. I was amazed by the number of paintings and sculpture that featured nude or semi-nude women either dead or dying. One of them that I remember in particular was a sculpture by David featuring a full size, completely nude woman stretched out over a log on her back with an arrow sticking out of her chest. I would like to know the necro fantasy behind that one!"

So, if you are comfortable with the themes of fantasy erotic horror, death, and handling of naked female bodies, please come in and sample what the site has to offer:

Hank
and
JohnM

[Club Dead Store] [Model Pages] [Stories] [Links] [Forum] [Coming Attractions] [Pay Per View]

E-mail to Club-Dead

23373

Return to Entry Page

Plate 2b Club-Dead homepage, January 2000

still in the red but people pay for erotic content probably in billions of dollars per year. The money is helping to build the Internet in every way ... technology, infrastructure, business models.

Bizarre instructs its readers on the most exciting sites such as www.necrobabes.com; www.ruemorgue.com; or www.torture.net, whose homepage explains

> Real sex and violence, banned material, uncensored and uncut footage of everything that you were told is wrong. Inside you will find scenes of gore, violence, rape, snuff, hanging, dead bodies, genital mutilation, aborted babies, suicides, necrophilia, dead celebrities, murder victims, autopsy photography and much, much, more.

Club-Dead, visited each month by tens of thousands of consumers, makes claims to be about erotic art but a cursory glance at its video 'menu', with descriptions of 'extreme violence' and 'rape', are evidence enough of the pleasures it is peddling with its emphasis on appearing as real as possible (see Plates 2a, 2b). And as *Bizarre* adds, 'all for free, which is very nice'. Again we have the merging of the promise of reality with wrongness and the actual production of pain for the consumption not just for a minority but for millions world-wide. Once more the process of the consumption of the commodity, in this case the commodity of entertainment, masks the pain involved in the process of production.

The enjoyment of cruelty continues with www.collide-ascope.com which shows a film clip of a car running over a pigeon as well as crushed frogs and rabbits etc. And *Bizarre* informs us that gorezone.com has an image of 'a women run over by a large bus with her brains extracted' as well as 'pictures of disembowelled bodies and murder victims'. And there are well-attended sites for other transgressive pleasures such as www.cockfight.com plus all the news on bare-knuckle fighting and dog-fighting.

How then can we begin to make sense of this growing

production of violence and humiliation as entertainment? As I have already argued, as the civilising process advances and places new constraints on social behaviour, then new irrational consumer goods appear. At the same time the process of commodification relies upon the efficiency of production and efficiency in everyday life. As science and rationality attempt to order everyday life and meanings, so irrationality is banished into the process of consumption as irrational acts become a commodity in themselves, acting as a bridge to the displaced world of the 'upside-down'. In the grey world of order, the violence and cruelty of contemporary reality television and other media may be a bridge to a displaced world of irrationality and chance where our subjectivity runs riot. It is these dual forces of a post-modern society that are at work here, where commodification and scientific rationality combine to create an explosive 'self-destructive cocktail of capitalism', where the individual's identity implodes into the secret and carnivalesque 'second life', and where all that is transgressive and irrational resides.

6   The criminalisation of consent: the case of S&M

In 1987 the sexual activities of a group of gay men in England came to the notice of the local police who suspected they had by chance discovered an organised group of violent men in the snuff movie business. This was seen as a veritable satanic circle of depraved homosexuals who were a threat to society in general and who were put under surveillance via what the police named 'Operation Spanner'. This was the stuff that all police and politicians dream about: protecting the weak from the strong; the moral from the immoral; the orderly from the disorderly. The result was that 42 people were arrested, of whom 16 were prosecuted and eventually charged with a number of offences including assault, aiding and abetting, and keeping a disorderly house because they had been found to be involved in consensual sadomasochistic sexual practices, including genital piercings and branding with hot wires. At the end of the court case in 1990, 15 were convicted (losing appeals in 1992 at the Court of Appeals and in 1993 at the House of Lords). Three defendants (Tony Brown, Roland Jaggard and Colin Laskey) eventually took their cases to the European Court who, in upholding the British court's original decision, completed the process of the criminalisation of a specific popular form of sexual expression amongst consenting adults. Society was saved (see Morton 1999)!

Any discussion concerning sexual behaviour comes loaded with pitfalls and problems; a veritable minefield of mistakes. This is even more the case when that behaviour contains within it the possibility of pain and humiliation, albeit for the purposes of pleasure and always consensual. But when we have millions of citizens throughout the Western world who are in some way involved in the pleasurable world of S&M (sadomasochism) sex play, then we need at least to be brave enough to enter the minefield and endeavour to make sense of what we see. It is always easier to attempt to grasp the past rather than the present but if sociology has anything to offer, then this lies in its ability to make sense of the 'here and now' of any social behaviour, including sexual behaviour. If sociology is unable to attempt even that, then it seems to have little to offer. And it is obvious that forms of S&M practices no longer constitute a subculture but are becoming more and more a part of acceptable everyday life.

The activities in recent years of both the British courts and police have resulted in the successful criminalising of the sexual play of consenting citizens, whilst non-consenting violence (normally towards children or in sport) remains legal. Although there has been some flexibility in the approach of the courts both in Britain and elsewhere in recent years (e.g. *Regina* vs *Wilson* and *Regina* vs *Church* in Britain; the Christopher McIntosh case in the state of Victoria in Australia; *Boldt* vs *Boldt* in the USA), the message remains quite clear that S&M sex is still illegal in England and Wales and elsewhere. If McClintock (1993) is correct, then it is not difficult to understand why. She clearly asserts that S&M is the world upside-down *par excellence* in that it reverses all the logic and rationality of liberal society, thus becoming not only carnivalesque in nature but also oppositional to the existing political and social power relations of conventional society. This helps to explain why there have been such strenuous efforts by the regulatory forces of society to oppress and criminalise such behaviour. As a fragmentation of carnival it can contain the obscene, the obscure and the grotesque. It is both about the beauty and the exercise of power as well as the beauty of exercising power in a truly upside-down bottom-up society, where judges are judged and ultimately punished, the powerful dispossessed and demanded of rather than demanding. And all within the context of consent, desire and pleasure.

There can be little doubt of the growing popularity of cultural forms of S&M activities that have seen it move from the domain of 'art' into the realm of the everyday. The filmmakers have long dealt with the topic throughout the history of film. Notable films in the last few decades include Richard Michael's *The Berlin Affair* (1970), Lucio Fulci's *A Lizard in Woman's Skin* (1971) (orig. *Una lucertola con le pelle de donna*), Lilliana Cavani's *Night Porter* (1973) and *Beyond Good and Evil* (1984), David Lynch's *Blue Velvet* (1986), Adrian Lyne's *9½ Weeks* (1986), David Cronenberg's *Crash* (1996) and Kirby Dick's *Sick: The Life and Death of Bob Flanagan, Supermasochist* (1997). The latter won the Sundance Film Festival special prize and was shown at the Edinburgh Film Festival as well as being seen by the public at large on general release. The film *Romance*, directed by Catherine Breillat in 1999, is the latest in the genre to attract attention. In an interview with the *Sunday Times* Breillat exclaimed, 'Sex is always mental', which was why she felt she could justify the sadomasochistic bondage sequences in the film where the character Marie, in her quest for her sexual soul, has a rape fantasy made flesh and crosses that pain–pleasure threshold with a much older, unattractive and sadistic man. Was that, the interviewer wondered, from experience too? The reply came, 'Well, the mental side of feeling sexual towards something ugly is universal' (*Sunday Times* 26/9/99). And back in 1941 Orwell talked of 'a sort of sub-world of smacked bottoms ... which is part of western European consciousness' (Orwell 1941: 144). Performance art has of course always had strong S&M connections with its references to bodily alterations.

Texts of both the analysis of and fictional stories about S&M abound and are all readily available from everyday newsagents or booksellers. In addition a surge of 'How to' publications have emerged. Anita Phillips' *A Defence of Masochism* (Faber 1998) (in which she states that masochism is a very intelligent perversion) is one such example of an attempt at analysis. *Screw the Roses, Send Me the Thorns* by Philip Miller and Mollie Devon (Mystic Rose Books 1998) is a 'How to' book, and Brame *et al. Different Loving: The World of Sexual Dominance and Submission* (Century 1997) is a mixture of both. The extent of the popularity of all kinds of publication of this type was clearly seen in the Canterbury branch of Waterstones' bookshop in January 1999, when its window display had the theme of GO TO BED WITH A BOOK and included a collection of Taschen publications such as *Elmer Batters, New York Girls, Fetish Girls*, plus complete collections of *Bizarre, Erotic Universales, Exotique, The Story of O* and *The Dominant Wives and Other Stories* by Eric Stanton. Their window was a riot of oral and anal sex, erect penises and enlarged clitorises, rubber wear, handcuffs and chains, canes, whips and women urinating on men. Nobody batted an eyelid and all the publications were gathered together for sale on one table inside the store making the average Soho book shop look boring. In Canterbury at least S&M is not on the 'top shelf' but is firmly rooted in the 'everyday', in the everyday lives of its population.

In the magazine sector *Skin Two*, based in London, is one of the most respected publications on the international S&M scene. It fully details both UK and international activities, clubs and associations, as well as acting as a showcase for S&M commodities. Its images come from the aesthetics of high fashion and art photography, with an editorial group that talks of Oxbridge days and doctoral theses. It publishes over 25,000 copies quarterly and has a readership of over 50,000. More startling is its web site that, with more than 60,000 hits a day, is visited more often than the BBC's. *Skin Two*'s annual 'Rubber Ball' sells over 3,500 tickets, is televised to a number of countries and is supported by a host of celebrities such as Jean Paul Gaultier and Mick Jagger. It is therefore both popular and celebrated. More everyday magazines, such as *Bizarre*, with its circulation of 100,000 and readership of half a million, are essentially concerned with a mixture of sex and violence and in doing so play on the fringes of S&M. (See *Bizarre* Oct. '98, 'Is it about sex and violence?' 'Yea, absolutely'. Interview with Kathy Poole, editorial.)

Indeed the whole new generation of contemporary men's magazines, *Sky*, *Front*, *Stuff*, *Deluxe* and *Maxim* all dabble with popular images of S&M (for example *Loaded*'s Feb. 1999 issue on flagellation with a circulation of half a million and a readership of millions). *GQ*'s March 1999 issue claimed to be about 'Sex and Violence' (see Plate 3) and had various poses by model Caprice with chains, crops and hand-cuffs. (The editor left after this issue not because of S&M images but for a feature depicting Nazi officials and generals as amongst the most stylish men of the twentieth century.) Even *Men's Health* magazine made a fun attempt at connecting healthy sex with 'pervery' when in its May 1999 issue under the heading, 'Tonight's plan of action', it stated: 'Surprise her by exploring new and erotic sexual territory (but it's probably wise to leave the handcuffs, custard and giant nappies till, say, the third or fourth go).'

In the area of advertising, promotions have for some time used references to the S&M culture, as exemplified by Linda Evangelista in Yardley's S&M campaign, handcuffed yet happy selling lipstick! Lee jeans, with its ad featuring a stiletto heel on a bare back, continued the S&M theme whilst it must have been almost demanded by Gucci shoes that they would use foot fetish images in their adverts. Even Bass beers used S&M images in its 1997 sales campaign linking the licking of the Dominatrix boot to the drinking of beer, whilst the simple adverts for the Iron Bed Company (see Plate 4) hidden away in the mass adverts of the weekend newspapers exclaims 'Some people are asking to be slapped behind bars' followed later by 'Men shouldn't be chained to the kitchen sink'. Virgin Radio continued the brass bed and handcuffs theme (see Plate 5) whilst Altoid drew on classic Betty Page images with its 1999 advert that simply stated that there is 'Pleasure in Pain'. In America, *Time Out New York* magazine managed in 1998 to have one edition dedicated to the S&M scene detailing specialist clubs and eateries whilst almost all other major international cities seem to boast at least one

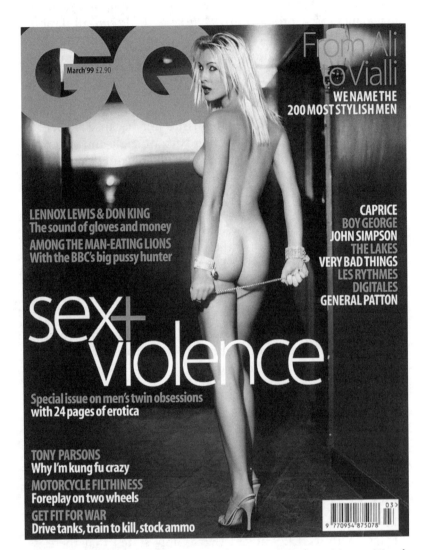

Plate 3 GQ magazine front cover of 'Sex and Violence' issue, March 1999 (Condé Nast publications)

Plate 4 Iron Bed Company advert 1999/2000 (Saatchi & Saatchi advertising agency)

Plate 5 Virgin Radio advert 1999 (Duckworth Finn Grubb Waters advertising agency)

S&M restaurant if not more. In Britain S&M clubs thrive not only in the big cities of Brighton and London but also in Colchester, Cornwall, Western-super-Mare and Leeds as the meanings of S&M become slowly integrated into both popular culture and the carnivalesque.

Bodily alterations as an everyday activity are both widely popular and widely practised. Now every town in Britain has its own 'piercing' parlour, which no longer restricts itself to simple ear piercing but lists the delights of tongue, nipple, penis and clitoral adornments (see Plate 6). Companies such as Metal Morphosis in London have their own fully portable body-piercing surgery that gets to places others can't reach to pierce that which others can't reach. Erotic piercing is now commonplace. The connections between piercing, tattooing and sexuality are made visible in magazines such as *Savage* and *Secret*. No longer are these fringe activities; they are part of the everyday existence of large proportions of young people who are growing up playing with the sexual stimulation of S&M. Metal Morphosis estimate that there are 40–50 specialist 'piercers' in London alone, achieving up to 2,500 piercings a week between them. Many of these piercings are not simply body jewellery but 'significantly affect bodily sensations during sex or otherwise' (Curry 1993: 72). And 'in this sense . . . might be said to lead to the creation of new sensations and pleasures outside of the reality of normalised sexual discourse' (Sweetman 1997: 2).

Navel piercing is still at the moment the most popular, although some 600 genital piercings a week are being performed in the London area alone, with a 50/50 gender split. This could only mean that there are thousands of erotic piercings being completed weekly throughout Britain, yet the anomaly remains that you can pay to be pierced by a professional piercer but it remains illegal to be pierced in private by a friend. The professional process, as does the private process, 'necessarily involves pain, blood, and the penetration of the skin in a non medicalised setting' (Sweetman 1997: 2); a setting, it may be added, where it is illegal to use an anaesthetic. But there is little doubt that piercing is already a large

TONGUE:
Healing Time 2 - 3 months
Very popular but not all tongues are piercable.

EARL:
Healing Time
Usually grows out please consult a piercer for more information.

MADISON:
Healing Time
Usually grows out please consult a piercer for more information.

NUCHAE:
Healing Time
Usually grows out please consult a piercer for more information.

PRINCE ALBERT:
Healing Time 2 - 3 months.
Very popular, again not all can be pierced. Very easy to heal.

GUICHE:
Healing Time 3 - 5 MONTHS
Can be hard to heal and dislikes irritation.

FRENUM:
Healing Time 2 - 3 MONTHS
Easy to heal and can sometimes grow out.

HAFADA:
Healing Time 2 - 4 MONTHS
Easy to heal simple piercing.

FORESKIN:
Healing Time 2 - 3 MONTHS
Easy to heal.

INNER LABIA:
Healing Time 6 WEEKS - 2 MONTHS.
Easy to heal, settles very quickly.

OUTER LABIA:
Healing Time 2 - 3 MONTHS
Easy to heal, settles very quickly.

CLITORIS HOOD:
Healing Time 2 - 3 MONTHS
Very popular and easy to care for.

MALE GENITAL PIERCING

	STAINLESS STEEL	NIOBIUM
PRINCE ALBERT	£35.00	£52.00
✱ GUICHE WITH RING	£30.00	£45.00
GUICHE WITH BARBELL	£35.00	
PUBIC WITH RING	£30.00	£45.00
PUBIC WITH BARBELL	£30.00	
✱ FRENUM WITH RING	£30.00	£40.00
FRENUM WITH BAR	£30.00	
HAFADA (SCROTUM) WITH RING	£30.00	£45.00
HAFADA WITH BAR	£30.00	
FORSKIN	£30.00	£45.00

FEMALE GENITAL PIERCING

	STAINLESS STEEL	NIOBIUM
INNER LABIA	£30.00	£40.00
OUTER LABIA	£30.00	£40.00
PREPUCE (CLITORIS HOOD) HORIZONTAL OR VERTICAL	£30.00	£40.00
CLITORIS HOOD (WITH BAR)	£35.00	

SPECIAL GOLD PRICES

PRICES INCLUDE PIERCING & JEWELLERY

18CT GOLD RING FROM	£56.00
18CT GOLD BARBELL FROM	£63.00
18CT GOLD BANANA BELL FROM	£127.00
18CT GOLD JEWELLED BANANA BELL FROM	£120.00
18CT GOLD CUBIC ZIRCONIUM BANANA BELL FROM	£108.00

LARGE RANGE OF 9 & 18CT JEWELLERY

£5.00 DEPOSIT IS REQUIRED FOR ALL BOOKINGS.

A MINIMUM OF 48 HOURS NOTICE IS REQUESTED FOR CANCELLATION OR CHANGE OF APPOINTMENT TIME.

Plate 6 Metal Morphosis piercing menu

and still unregulated industry producing a product that involves both sexual pleasure and pain. It is clear that to pierce for profit rather than for mutual pleasure is still more acceptable to the law.

The latest bodily alterations for pleasure are the application of 'designer scars'. One surgeon is reported in the *Sunday Times* as saying 'My fellow surgeons are willing to cut the body in all sorts of bizarre ways in the name of fashion, inserting alien substances into lips and breasts. By comparison, a small healthy scar on the cheek seems a tiny price to pay for someone's idea of beauty' (*Sunday Times* 29/9/99).

There can be little doubt from this brief thumbnail sketch of popular tastes that S&M activities are now firmly embedded in the cultural fabric of everyday life at an international level and have become part of the consciousness and lived life of millions of citizens. The question then arises as to how such a popular activity is still subjected to the social processes of criminalisation and demonisation. Or more generally, how is it that the popular becomes criminal?

S&M is still regarded as a pathology of the mind and has been part of the psychiatrising of delinquency that began in the nineteenth century starting with:

necrophilia	1840
kleptomania	1860
homosexuality	1869 (criminalised 1887)
exhibitionism	1876
psychopathia sexualis (sado-masochism)	1886 (criminalised 1993)
narcissism	1898

(Tambling 1990)

S&M is still on a World Health Organization list of mental disorders and yet, as Thompson (1994) concludes in his excellent account of the whole S&M question, 'After 70 years of failing to collect any decent empirical data about sadomasochism, psychiatric knowledge of sadomasochism is non existent' (Thompson 1994: 65). The results of the plethora of explanations delivered over the last hundred years has acted only to bury and mystify the reality of S&M practices more deeply. For many, men are the natural pathological passive victims and for others, such as Krafft-Ebing (1947), they are the natural pathological aggressors. For Ellis (1942) there is the notion of masochism and love, whilst Hirschfield proposes the idea of 'stimulation craving' rather than 'pain craving' (Thompson 1994). The reality is that there is a complexity of heightened interrelating emotions that are 'discharged' through sensual sex. Historically, sexuality has always been a topic 'for discussion through confession' thereby connecting sexuality with wrong-doing and so punishment and pain. By reversing this, punishment and pain justify the sexual and become pleasurable and desired (Tambling 1990). Confessing our transgressions has become a great entertainment/play commodity as punishment so often was in the past (see Ch. 5). So it is not remarkable that the world of S&M and other extreme pleasures is often the world of confession, punishment and pleasure woven together to become the commodification of confession and the consumption of pain. Indeed, the whole concept of giving and receiving pain remains confused in contemporary British society, hence the approach to the 'smacking' of children as supported by the Prime Minister Tony Blair in 1998 and the public's dismay at the possibility of losing this 'right'. The Internet web sites concerned with the corporal punishment debate are extensive and almost always directly connected to religious beliefs (Cook 1994). In recent years there has been considerable public interest in the caning of Westerners in places such as Singapore, and there seems always to be a market for stories about floggings and executions in the Middle East region, be it of nationals or Westerners, men or women. As Nietzsche remarked, it seems that 'only that which goes on hurting will stay in the memory' (cited in Stanley 1996: 169).

But it is Foucault who begins to hint historically of the power relationships involved in both punishment by the State and in S&M practices (which he himself became involved with later in his life) when he remarked that 'it might be said

that all knowledge is linked to the essential forms of cruelty'
(Stanley 1996: 169). In this way playing with power becomes
an essential ingredient of S&M consensual play. It would be
wrong though to equate this simply with patriarchal power,
for it seems in practice that there are women who dominate
men; men women; women women; and men men.

> A common mistake is that women aren't into it and are
> just pleasing their boyfriends. The ultimate icon of the
> S&M movement is a women fully in charge with desires
> who knows what she wants and goes and gets it and
> whether she's dominant to men or women, she's a
> dominant icon. Women who are dominant in their sexual-
> ity ... in fetish clubs is 50/50 or biased towards
> women. . . .
>
> I've run women's parties for 35–40 women, all women
> on their own, not a man in sight. They're the dirtiest, you
> know, hard-core parties that you ever get on the S&M
> scene when a load of women get together and decide to do
> rude things to each other. It's a load of women making
> their own fun. Women are very creatively perverse on
> their own without men being involved.
>
> Then there's the aspect of submissive women, which
> is much harder to explain ... especially when dominated
> by a man. There again these are women for whom
> playing submissive sexual roles and S&M games is
> what gets them off, they get turned on by doing that
> and again within a fetish relationship or S&M club
> scenario these women can get what they want, which is
> to be submissive within the parameters of that sort of
> relationship. . . .
>
> What do women get from being submissive? The
> answer is they get what they want. If you want to be
> submissive you should be able to stand up and say 'Tie
> me up I love it'. It requires being very strong to be a
> submissive. Being submissive does not equal being weak.
>
> (Interview with Lisa Sherman, practising dominant
> and editor of *Skin Two*)

Here Lisa is at pains to stress the power that she feels women have, or ought to have, in expressing their own sexuality. She went on to discuss the edgework involved in taking consenting partners to the limits and the boundaries of self-regulation and then on to the very edge of transgression, boundary-breaking and the shame of doing wrong.

> Submissive women are often after asking people to push them past their physical and emotional limits, be it humiliation play or pain play. It's the overcoming of personal limits like an athlete.
>
> The dominant person needs the submissive's adulation and respect. To achieve that you need to push them to the edge. It's about head sex ... My friends are serious players. One's a second-hand car dealer from Kent, another's a professor. We like being on the edge ... Underground.
>
> (Interview with Lisa Sherman, *Skin Two*)

Yet all this is viewed as everyday and ordinary – as part of the sexual vocabulary of the majority of society rather than of the obscure or simply the domain of men. It is seen to be part of a 'new' notion of 'girl power' that is reflected throughout the media, where women can talk about 'shagging' as much as men, talk about their sexuality as much as men, their fantasies and their transgressions as much as men. To celebrate them whenever they can, wherever they can and to be seen to be as outrageous, if not more so, as they can. For 'girl power' there is no sexual oppression, just individual needs, desires and pleasures to be fulfilled come what may. Whether this is at all so or whether this is a conspiratorial construction between men and the media is something yet to become clear. However, what is apparent and visible is the extent of the carnivalesque pleasures enjoyed by many women and men which are profoundly different in style to those of the past. Carnival has 'come out' and in so doing will come into conflict with the aspirations and fantasies of the State. That is political conflict. As Cavani remarks, there is always a distinction between pornography and eroticism based on aesthetic choice which always involves the political (Cavani 1977).

> It's not obscure . . . if you feel different when you put on different clothes . . . say sexy clothes or black, then you have an element of 'perve' in you . . . you have a fetish. Far more than 50 per cent of the population have these feelings for say shiny black.
> (Interview with Tim Woodward, editor, *Skin Two*)

However for the State the gendering of S&M happens through the discourses of deviancy, science and rationality rather than through the discourses of sexuality, thereby rendering women as able as men to be deviant and/or sexually pathological and to be either bad, mentally ill or both. Within the discourse of the 'deviant' and the 'sick' there can be no room for mutual relationships to exist from which the idea of consent and harmless play could spring. The deviants don't wait for consent; the mentally ill are unable to give it. In other words S&M activities are, for the State, seen to be about coercion, victims, violence and evil. It is evidence of a sickness in society that can only and must only result in protective legal action, part of which is to outlaw and criminalise consent for the good of society and in the interest of the people. As Lord Templeman stated in his Spanner Appeal ruling in the House of Lords, 'Society is entitled and bound to protect itself against a cult of violence. Pleasure derived from the infliction of pain is an evil thing. Cruelty is uncivilised.' And so it is, but it is not a part of S&M pleasurable play. Famous serial killers do not get consent from victims. Brady and Hindley did not have a S&M relationship. Like the Wests they practised their cruelty on others not themselves. They had no consensual partners only coerced victims and as such had absolutely nothing to do with S&M activities. For judges to think so showed only ignorance and social blindness. As always, the law was attempting to regulate the everyday of the past.

For those whose lives involve S&M the complete opposite is true. Consent and trust and rules within relationships are paramount. To break a rule is to break trust and therefore consent. As Lynn Chancer has pointed out (1992), S&M is based on extreme need and a trust that we might not find in wider society, nor indeed (as in Genet's play *The Balcony*), in the actions of judges and the law. She goes on to explain that it is about 'pleasure diversity and consenting mutual self-exploration'.

> It's not violent [S&M] . . . I am not a violent type. On the issue of consent and harm. . . . There is no distress that you would find as in the caning of children. You need two to make S&M. It's not S&M without exchange . . . without consent. For consent to be valid it must be given by an adult who is not under the influence of anything, be it drugs, alcohol, love or just bad judgement. If you've had a few beers just forget it. You must have rules just like if you take up flying or motor racing or sub-aqua . . . you don't ride a motor bike without a helmet. And so you never restrict breathing or use manacles with different keys. There's no problems with rules.
>
> (Interview with Tim Woodward, editor *Skin Two*)

The consent/coercion controversy is an important aspect of S&M life. If S&M is no more than pleasurable erotic play, then why should we or judges think that the players are any more coerced than, say, the actresses and actors playing victims in *Pulp Fiction* are coerced to play and act out violence?

The State, in controlling the official meanings of and responses to violence, is free to make exceptions to its laws of assault, as in sporting or national security and military activities. The whole area of the laws of assault is confused and complex in its interpretation. However the question of motivation, that is the reason for violence, is a central concern. Put simply, the State cannot allow us to live in a violence-free society. No matter the rhetoric of politicians concerning violence and being violent, it is nevertheless viewed as a political necessity to have our ability to be violent kept in a continual state of readiness for the protection of society. That is of course the readiness of men for war. Violence must, under the law, offer some 'manly' wartime skills (Thompson 1994: 220) and it is in the realm of sport that those skills are found. The act of 'maiming' was originally the act of rendering another person unable to 'fight' for their State. In other words the body belongs to the State and is protected by the State through the laws of assault to ensure that the machine of war is kept intact and ready for acceptable violence. At this point acceptable violence, for the State, ceases to exist. It is made invisible and as such no longer exists in reality but exists only in an ideological vacuum specifically created by the law (Thompson 1994). In his Spanner judgment in the House of Lords, Lord Templeman defined S&M sex as real violence and blows struck in sport as not, as ideological violence. He judged that consent cannot be a defence where there is intent 'to do corporal hurt' (Justice Cave) or indeed when blows are to be struck in anger. Lord Templeman listed a number of violent acts as lawful such as male circumcision, tattooing, ear piercing and violent sports including boxing (Morton 1999: 237). The motivation for violence was for the Court of Appeal of central importance.

> It is not in the public interest . . . that people should try to cause, or should cause, each other actual bodily harm for no good reason . . . what may be good reason it is not necessary for us to decide. It is sufficient today . . . that sado-masochistic libido does not come within the category of 'good reason'.

Once more Lord Templeman in the Spanner Appeal highlighted the motivational aspects of violence when he stated that 'the violence of sadists and the degradation of their victims have sexual motivations, but sex is no excuse for violence'. He concluded: 'I am not prepared to invent a defence of consent for sado-masochistic encounters which breed and glorify cruelty and result in offences'. But in the eyes of the law, violence for the State is an acceptable excuse. The notion apparently held by the judges that sport is free of hate and its only motivation is to make sports people ready and able to fight for one's country (State), seems not just dubious but pathetically ludicrous. One can only wonder which sports the judges have any experience of, or indeed whether they are still reading *The Tough of the Track*! But there is the veiling of violence by the law in cases such as *R* vs *Ciccarelli*, where one of the most violent sports, that of ice hockey, was deemed to contain only consensual violence for all to enjoy. This has now conclusively been judged to be the realm of 'manly' activities and therefore is both a useful and desirable activity. We need not even contemplate the role and practices of contemporary boxing to understand the continuing support that the law gives in promoting violence for profit. And I doubt whether simply by agreeing to play sport we really consent to have violence done to us – our skulls cracked, legs broken, faces punched, all in the pursuit of profit. (It is interesting to note that in a recent case in the Victoria Supreme Court in Australia Justice Frank Vincent ruled that activities involving the application of physical force involving the risk of injury were not against state law since 'if that were the case many sporting contests would become unlawful'.)

If just by going into a sports arena, or underground station, or supermarket, you are consenting to being 'battered', then why not the dungeon? Whilst the regulation of sexuality continues to be a major concern of politicians and the law, so contemporary sexual practices will continue to be 'outlawed'. Home Secretaries who create laws also create crime. In this case the innocent sexual activities of many have been criminalised by stealth and legal process. 'Thus an activity is criminalised, without any reference to Parliament, and the statistical crime wave is impelled ever onwards' (*The Times* 20/12/1990; cited in Thompson 1994: 261).

Sex was something that was a part of our unspoken lives. Like our everyday personal relationships it existed: not taken for granted but simply untalked about and un-remarked on. It hung there in our consciouness; part of our minds and part of our bodies; yet separated out from the family as firmly part of the personal. It flashed into life occasionally when grandad got overly excited about the Tiller Girls dance troupe on television, or when mum and dad giggled in the bath together. I, like everyone else, gleaned my sexuality from what was around me, the Church, the Classics, Art and school. Sex, to be talked about or seen, had to be positioned as part of the practices of the past. It couldn't be contemporary because we were young and it was forbidden to soil our innocence, it could only come from the past. Mainly I seemed to have been surrounded by images of nakedness and suffering. Greek myths seemed to be about half-naked people chained to rocks being tortured by the gods. In church we sang about the ecstasy of suffering as we viewed the flesh of the martyrs being scourged for God. By God for God it all seemed the same to me.

Sunday was sex day as we chanted and celebrated the pain and passion suffered by the Saints. Around us the sun shone through the stained glass windows showing the passion of pain, the agony and the ecstasy, all woven into a dense tapestry of sex where nudity, blood, chains, whips, pain and pleasure seemed the central goal of what we should desire from life. All the martyrs, men and women, seemed beautiful to me, their deep crimson marks of suffering contrasting against their white muscu-lar bodies. It was all deeply rich in sound, colour and theatre and was very confusing. In school the sex life of rabbits, served up in Science, was never going to be a serious threat to the colour, excitement and sensualness of the sexuality of the past.

(Presdee 1988)

7 Rap and rave and the criminalisation of youth

Now youth the hour of thy dread passion comes
thy lovely things must all be laid away
(Ivor Gurney, 'To the Poet in Battle', 1915)

One of the enduring myths of political and social life is the one that sees young people as being the central cause of forms of crime and disorder that strike at the very heart of the stability and prosperity of contemporary social life. It is a convenient myth that both constructs and brings into social being the image of 'criminal youth' (Muncie 1999) to be feared, distrusted, puzzled over and forever surveyed. Almost every week we agonise over the downward moral spiral of our young as they are seen by the media to plunge ever further into the depths of violence and incomprehensible and dangerous black humour. Each death in a school in America, such as the 'Trench coat' gang massacre in Denver, sparks a new debate about youth in Britain. For politicians and public alike there lies in this 'simple' construction a correspondingly 'simple' and thereby recognisable 'truth' that we all appear enthusiastically and willingly to grasp. It is a simplistic premise that places young people as the major cause of the 'cracks' in capitalism. This leads to the belief that there are and must be correspondingly simple political and social remedies that can be aimed at controlling young people in order to 'care' for capitalism. Along with this enduring myth

is the corresponding enduring practical process of the criminalisation of young people which maintains the never-ending
reconstruction of young people as 'the devils of the street'.

There is of course a collective confusion within adult society about what it is to be young or to be a 'youth'. As a society
we can't make up our minds whether there is such a psychological condition called adolescence in the first place, or
whether this is simply a socially constructed condition called
'youth'. We can't agree when it begins or when it ends. Does it
end at 10 years, when the law regards us as being responsible
for our sexual behaviour? Or is it 16 years, when the law
regards us as mature enough to 'have' sexual relationships?
Or is it 18 years, when the law regards us as able to watch
sexual activities at the cinema? Does it end at 18 years when
the Children's Act ceases to consider us children? Or do we
remain 'youth' until 24 years, when Social Services deems us
to be of age and begins to provide adult unemployment benefits? Do we become adult at 12, 14 or 16 years, all ages when
the Child Support Agency insists that young men must pay
maintenance for any children they 'father'? Or is it at 19
years, when the Child Support Agency considers a young person's financial dependency on their parents comes to an end?
In reality we define 'youth' through cultural and political
practices that reflect the power and social structures that
already exist. The Millennium Dome national exhibition, setting the tone for the nation's next millennium, has already
banned all young people under the age of 16 not accompanied by an 'adult' from attending, fearing that young
people will run riot, thereby defining in practice young people
as unruly, irresponsible and excluded as individuals in their
own right. The new millennium carries on where the old left
off with the continuing demonisation of young people.

Cultural practices can be gleaned from such obscure artefacts as the Berlitz *French Vocabulary Handbook* (1994), the
sort of language dictionary which provides many people with
their first understandings of people from another place. This
is a publication where under 'Addiction and Violence' is the
entry 'skinhead' and 'punk' as well as the sentence: 'Many

young people have a drug problem. They start by sniffing solvents or by taking soft drugs. Cannabis is the most common' (p. 97). Here we have a quick and easy way of transporting prejudices about young people across national boundaries to continental Europe. The language dictionary goes on to explain that young people 'quickly become addicted. Then go on to hard drugs'.

Notwithstanding the imprecision of the meaning of the term, 'youth' has become a convenient category for political and social control policies that enable things to be 'done' to young people for no reason other than that they *are* young. It also enables politicians and adult society to 'do' things, be active, show you care, be involved and be good citizens. When you can't control adults, you can always control 'youth' and be applauded for it. When the Chancellor of the Exchequer Gordon Brown wanted to penalise those unemployed who wouldn't take 'badly' paid 'bad' work, he experimented first on young people who after refusing one job opportunity lost two weeks' benefit, after two refusals they lost four weeks' benefit and after three refusals, six months' benefit. A sort of three strikes and you're out of this society! It didn't seem to worry the Chancellor that there were hundreds of thousands of young people who had no legitimate income and that they might be forced by his policies to attain illegitimate income. In the end the State view seems to be that to discipline and to control 'youth' is to care for 'youth'. The battle 'against' rather than 'for' youth is seen as a war against disorder and immorality. This is a battleground into which young people in the daily practice of their 'everyday' lives enter in order to defend their space, their beliefs, their music, their morality.

Yet 'adult' society is continually confronted with a maze of social 'facts' about the often desperate social situation of young people. The 'think-tank' Demos now talks of another 'lost' generation as they look for and agonise over the 600,000 16- to 24-year-olds in Britain who are not involved in work, training or education. Then there are the 130,000 16- to 17-year-olds who make up the 'status zero' group, who again are not at work or in education or training and yet get no benefits either monetary or by way of schemes such as the New Deal for the unemployed, which only begins at 18. Added to this are 150,000 young people looking for work but not claiming benefits whilst a further 65,000 are not looking for work, not in education and training, not disabled and not caring for a dependant (Demos 1999). Here we have well over 300,000 young men and young women who appear to live and survive on no income at all. We could fill Wembley, our national football stadium, three times over just with impoverished young people whom we have excluded from the social and economic structures that provide for the rest of us an element of wealth and security. The often quoted figures of 5 million children living in poverty or the now one in three chance our children have of being born into poverty in the UK seem not to make any difference to our understanding of why 75 per cent of 16- to 17-year-old young men who are charged and appear before the youth courts are in no formal full-time activity (Social Exclusion Unit 1999). We reach not for understanding but moral indignation quickly followed by new control mechanisms, which include at the present time not only curfews and restraining orders but prison as well. Alongside our penchant for imprisoning more adults than the rest of the European Community, we also imprison more young people. We now detain 5,300 a year in England and Wales as against 16 in Denmark, 134 in Finland, 850 in Spain, 25 in Portugal and 8 in Sweden, with a 75 per cent rise in the three years to 1995 of 15- to 16-year-olds being remanded in custody.

Under the 'New Labour' government of Tony Blair the struggle to control young people totally continues alongside the continuing criminalisation of both childhood and the culture of young people. For this present Labour government no young person can be allowed to fall between the gaps of social policy. All have to be accounted for either in the custody of the family or under the control of the State, until the 'economy' calls for them to be released in an orderly fashion into the adult labour market. Work, or more likely training and the discipline for work, is seen as the antidote to crime whereas cultural behaviours such as cannabis use by young people are seen by the Home Secretary Jack Straw as a threat to the discipline for work, leading, he has suggested, to high rates of absenteeism (*Independent* 29/9/97). His 1998 Crime and Disorder Act, sections 14 and 15, criminalises children under 10 left unsupervised after 9.00pm. He thus casts himself in the role of State 'sandman', regulating both bedtime and methods of play. The inference is surely that all young people by this time ought to be either in bed or involved in adult-supervised educational activities rather than involved in meaningless unsupervised youthful pleasure and leisure. In August 1999 two 17-year-olds from Liverpool (*Guardian* 7/9/99) became the first young people to be banned from specific spaces using the new antisocial behaviour orders, as if a society creating half a million young people living in poverty wasn't antisocial in itself. Meanwhile in Rossendale, Lancashire, the local council has used these new government powers to impose a ban on using 'playgrounds' after 6.00pm in winter and 9.00pm in summer. Early in the millennium a boy of 12 became the youngest person to be 'excluded' from the town centre of Weston-super-Mare where he lived, having already been excluded from his school. This thereby introduced a sort of simple policy of 'house arrest' for youth (*The Times* 17/2/00).

These controlling mechanisms are mirrored in the United States, as the capital itself began, on 7 September 1999, a curfew for all those under 16 years of age who now had to be home by 11.00pm Sunday to Thursday and by midnight on Fridays and Saturdays. In Indiana young people must now have permission from parents for any 'body' procedure other than ear-piercing and in Tennessee they must be accompanied by an adult. Massachusetts recently attempted to prevent the sale of 'exotic' hair dyes, whilst Oklahoma had a try at banning tattoos.

The British courts continue to use the notion of 'youth' as a rationale for harsh punishments. When television presenter and personality Anthea Turner was caught speeding at

109 mph she was banned from driving for 4 weeks and fined £600, whilst David Horgan (29 years) who reached speeds of up to 133 mph was told by Justice Joseph Gosschalk: 'The message must go out to relatively *young* people that such high speeds on roads of that nature will be treated severely by the courts'. He was promptly jailed for 6 weeks and ordered to pay £400 (*Telegraph* 28/7/99). The message clearly was that being young added to an offence and to the sentence; this gave further credence to the notion that in modern Britain it is a crime to be young. Yet the latest national statistics for murder remind us how dangerous it is to be young, as the highest victim rate is for boys under the age of 1 year followed by young girls, and then by the 20–34 age range (Office for National Statistics 1999). Moreover in Northern Ireland the Civil Rights Bureau revealed that over 4,000 'children' under the age of 18 years had been directly affected by violence and that 189 'children', mainly in the age range 15–18, had been hospitalised after paramilitary beatings (*The Times* 17/9/99).

New Labour are not then about protecting the 'innocence' of the child as were the nineteenth-century child savers. For the Labour government there is no such thing as 'innocence', only responsibility and duty, as their abolition of *doli incapax* at the age of 10 (that a child is incapable of telling the difference between serious wrong and simple naughtiness) clearly shows. The New Labour government is about the taking on of more and more responsibility earlier and earlier. It is about discipline, work and assuming responsibility for your own actions from the age of 10, including responsibility for sexual behaviour. In September 1999 when Chancellor Gordon Brown made more severe his 'war on work-shy' young people (*The Times* 17/9/99), he remarked, 'It is now for young people to look at the one million vacancies and the opportunities that exist and show they have a responsibility to take them up'. Of course very few of the million job vacancies are in reality aimed at young people and the Chancellor would have known that. By shifting the blame for unemployment on to both young people themselves and their parents, he showed clearly that his policies weren't tough but cruel.

In July 1999 in two separate incidents, two young people were found guilty of indecent assault and were placed on the 'sex register' for varying periods of time. This procedure placed them alongside both persistent adult sex offenders who had abused young people as well as those who had raped. The first of these young offenders was a 10-year-old boy who was found guilty of assaulting an 8-year-old girl. The second was a 12-year-old girl who was found guilty of assaulting three boys aged 3, 4 and 5. In August of the same year the present British Prime Minister Tony Blair in response to two high-profile cases of teenage pregnancy (one where the father was 14, the other where the father was 23) embarked on a new moral campaign to save young people from the depravity of their modern lives. Blair promised more rules and regulations to be held over and against young people, a call that was a few days later supported publicly by the Home Secretary Jack Straw, who declared his determination to sweep the streets clean of youth. In an article in *The Times* newspaper, the Prime Minister clearly indicated that he was speaking for the newly discovered 'decent majority' in what appears to be no more than a pandering to the politics of the old 'moral majority'. He identified once more what he saw as the breeding-ground of future crime and disorder:

> A significant minority of children, often in sink estates, grows up amid deep family instability, poor education, endemic crime, drug abuse and few decent job opportunities. They are the ones likely to become the teenage mothers and fathers.
>
> (*The Times* 8/9/99)

Having identified the 'undeserving poor' as the source of crime etc. he went on to say:

> It is simply not acceptable for young children to be left without supervision, parental or otherwise, free to truant, vandalise and roam the streets at all hours. And it is

morally wrong for us to stand aside and to be indifferent
to it.

This of course justified in his mind the control mechanisms
that he had put in place that will either criminalise young
people or push them beyond the margins into the fourth
dimension of social life, where they become invisible to the
rest of society and its political processes; uncountable,
untouchable and unknowable and, most importantly, no
longer to be considered. And yet, paradoxically, to be 'outside of' society is central to most forms of youth culture. To be
pushed outside the perimeter of society and outside the
parameters of policy is precisely the aim of much youthful
behaviour in much the same way that to be sent outside of the
classroom for misbehaviour can be viewed by the 'miscreant';
that is, as a triumph rather than a humiliation.

The new truancy provisions of the Crime and Disorder Act
make every morning a roll-call for the control of youth, as the
police are given more power to take any young person of
school age (16 years) to a place of education or other designated area (sect. 16). The creation of a sort of youth 'pound'
in every town where parents can collect their children at the
end of the day is no more or less than the use of the police to
back up education policies that would fail without them. For
young people work becomes the 'gateway' to true civilisation
and citizenship, whereas leisure, pleasure and desire are the
'gateway' to savagery and nonlife.

Being 'young' is characterised by a culture created out of
the tensions that emanate between regulation and rebellion;
control and care; the civilised and the savage. The result is a
contesting carnivalesque culture that forever pushes at the
boundaries of transgression and where carnival becomes not
the 'second life of the people' but the first life of youth. Their
culture, rather than being a search for the 'authentic' as in
modern culture, is an endless search for the inauthentic; that
is, a culture that is empty of the authority and the imperatives
that come with authenticity. It is this perceived 'emptiness as
protest' that prompts panic from 'adult' society. As Deleuze

points out, 'negativity is all-pervasive' as it is throughout youth culture: 'Pure negation needs no foundation and is beyond all foundation, a primal delirium, an original and timeless chaos solely composed of wild and lacerating molecules' (Deleuze 1997: 27). It is a cultural chaos that can only appear unknowable to those 'outside', creating both fragmentation and fear.

Modern technology allows young people to create carnival all through the day as they fight to be visible and to be heard where of course they shouldn't. Now they carry their culture with them – the headphone and the mobile phone all giving instant communication, with defiance. You can be noisy yet silent in a library or a lesson, producing the ultimate attention-seeking upfront, in your face, defiant and occasionally 'really, really, resistant'. The silent nodding of the head to the music that no one else hears is like the silent 'tongue poking' and 'face pulling' of the past. It is the fragmentation and debris of carnival in the everyday lives of young people bringing music and talk into the world of silence; the world of disorder into the realms of order; the irrationality of emotion into the world of learning, rationality and science.

Music, whether it be in the making of it, communicating it, listening to it or simply moving to it, has always played an important part in the lives of young people and has had the ability to incense mainstream culture to the extent that there have always been attempts to control and criminalise it in some way. Writers as diverse as Plato, Adorno and Walter Benjamin have all discussed the power of music. At the turn of the century commentators in Australia often wrote of the ills of music and dancing.

> Larrikins love dancing above all human pleasures and indulge the passion whenever they find opportunity.
>
> (Pratt 1901)

> Young people frequent dancing saloons to their moral and spiritual detriment.
>
> (Mrs Burke; cited in the *Adelaide Advertiser* 25/5/1905)

The existence of dancing saloons is actually a menace to national life.

(Rev. Marsh; cited in the *Adelaide Advertiser* 25/4/1905)

Justice Rougier, presiding over a licensing law dispute in May 1999, showed that little had changed when he declared, 'This is the only country in the world where if you want to hold a dance you have to ask the police permission' (*Sunday Times* 16/5/99). Paying to dance on Sundays is only now being decriminalised in modern Britain.

In Nazi Germany in the 1930s regulations to control music-making were aimed at jazz as the music of ethnic impurity and degeneration. The regulations sought to control both the form of music and the emotions of those who listened to it.

1) Pieces in fox-trot rhythm (so-called swing) are not to exceed 20% of the repertoires of light orchestras and dance bands . . .

2) As to tempo . . . the pace must not exceed a certain degree of allegro, commensurate with the Aryan sense of discipline and moderation . . .

3) So-called jazz compositions may contain at most 10% syncopation; the remainder must consist of a natural legato movement devoid of the hysterical rhythmic reverses characteristic of the music of the barbarian races and conducive to dark instincts.

(Skvorecky 1980: 10)

This can be likened to the Criminal Justice and Public Order Act (1994) introduced by Michael Howard, then Home Secretary, who legislated against the making and listening to of rave music performed 'outside'. Of course he needed to be specific about the form of music itself so as not to outlaw the acceptable music of 'polite' society that abounds in the outdoors in any British summer such as that of the Glyndebourne Festival. He did so by criminalising both the producer and consumer of rave music which was identified in the Act as

' "music" [that] includes sounds wholly or predominantly characterised by the emission of a succession of repetitive beats' (sect. 63). The event could also be identified by the numbers of people that the Home Office felt made up a rave event: 'This section [63] applies to a gathering on land in the open air of 100 or more people (whether or not trespassers) at which amplified music is played during the night (with or without permission)'. However, this numerical concern criminalised both preparation and that very British institution the queue. People could be asked to disperse if:

a)   two or more persons are making preparations . . .
b)   ten or more persons are waiting for such a gathering to begin there.
c)   ten or more persons are attending such a gathering which is in progress.

(sect. 63)

If there were nothing oppositional or threatening about youthful music in all its forms, then there would be little point in forever fighting it. In other words, it is clear that youthful music does have an effect and that it resists and offends political forms and institutions in some way. It never has a 'nil' effect. It may dehumanise or be revolutionary; it may liberate or numb; it may question or seem empty, but it will always have an effect and offend the existing dominant culture in some way. It is part of the 'battle' that I talked of earlier, when young people engage in their defence of space and meaning, where they fight 'with music, drums like thunder, cymbals like lightening, banks of electric equipment like nuclear missiles of sound' (quoted in McKay 1998: 8). It is almost an intuitive understanding of the power of music that

in both simple and complex societies, it seems there is an awareness that the satisfaction of material needs tends to pull people apart from each other and it's often in music that they seek to repair the social damage.

(Martin 1995: 275)

This transgressive nature of music and its communication is evidenced by the extent to which measures are taken to control its production, distribution and consumption. Indeed the control over the communication airwaves are constant. The hijacking of airwaves is still seen as a gross act of piracy with pirate radio having a long, contentious and continuing history in this country. As in the case of the piracy of shipping, so piracy on the airwaves is dealt with harshly by the courts. In April 1999 Raymond Larmond was jailed for 28 days for illegally broadcasting his Flava FM radio station for more than a year and similar cases pepper the radio world of music. In the 1960s there was almost outright war declared against the famous pirates Radio Caroline and Radio London. This piracy has now spread to the Internet.

In a sense the whole world of youth subcultures has turned the rhythm of life upside-down. Whereas 30 years ago leisure and pleasure stopped, like Cinderella, at midnight, now pleasure doesn't start until midnight when the fun begins and often only ends when the weekend finishes. In the same way that truants often truant for no reason other than to stand outside of the rules, regulations and regimentation of life, so the 'weekend' becomes the process of the stretching of sensation. To 'buzz' is to be beyond, untouchable, an outsider. As such it is feared by the ordered and rational world of others. And the struggle over the control of music and movement is central to this part of life.

This struggle around music is the struggle between the performer who wants to create an impermanent sound that needs to be recreated time and time again, and the consumer who wants to possess it, own it and continually consume it. The technology of recording separated performer from the 'sound' and the video reunited performer and their music once more. Modern technology has separated it again as the technician becomes the performer, where the 'mix master' becomes the music-maker rather than the musician. This is what Frith calls the 'truth of music' (Frith 1986) and is the carnivalesque nature of club music, turning on its head as it does the accepted relationship between musician as the producer of music and technician as simply the transcriber of true sound. It is as if the 'sound' as the main experience is too precious a commodity to be left in the possession of performers. The sound seems to have become democratised through the process of mass consumption with the performers no longer being the 'stars'. Sound becomes in contemporary culture a 'natural' phenomenon belonging to all as the technicians become the harvesters of sound and as such the new 'stars' of music. To have a Ministry of Sound would not now seem far-fetched to the world of 'club land', where the mixer as musician talks music and the audience answers by dancing, creating a discourse where the mixer is the ruler of the genre and the 'raver' the possessed (Rouget 1990: 238).

What has happened in the world of music is the opposite to that which Benjamin had hoped for, where the age of mechanisation would liberate art in the same way that it would liberate people. Rather than becoming liberated from mechanisation, the art of modern music now lies in the mechanisation itself, in the machine, in the technology. Rather than technology freeing us to become human, technology has become the expression of humanness (Benjamin 1955: 227–228).

The modern nightclub industry is now worth well over £2 billion a year with over a million young people spending in excess of £35 per week on this form of pleasure (Malbon 1998: 266). Many pubs magically turn into nightclubs after the 'witching hour' has passed. Barmen become doormen, bouncers appear and club land begins. The whole style and process of 'clubbing' defies the rational scientific world of work which is held dream-like in the mind in contrast to the 'memories of a hedonistic consumption during the leisure hours' (Brake 1990: 75). It is a celebration of irrational ecstatic behaviour. Night becomes day and specialist clothes are worn not to work but to play. Consumption rather than production is all-important as the positive personal assessment of pleasure by the pleasured assumes the 'same qualities which were assessed negatively by their daytime controllers – e.g. laziness, arrogance, vanity, etc.' All 'positively defined by themselves and their peers in leisure time', as Hebdige (1998) puts it. It is the carnival of 'otherness', of 'difference' and defiance.

As there is niche marketing so there is niche music, as each club offers its own particular music to particular groups of people, creating their own anthems for 'doomed youth'. And still the notion of 'partying', criminalised by the Criminal Justice and Public Order Act (1994), remains central to club life. The mystique of the happening, the spectacle, the rave, continues as 'flyers' continue to be the important invitation to a party, indeed 'to party' all night, all weekend, all holiday. The free party scene is still going strong as clubbers seek out the unregulated carnivalesque atmosphere of the largely illegal free party.

Yet the fragmentation of 'rave' is like the fragmentation of carnival. Not only does it challenge the dominant forms of control but also other subcultural forms (McKay 1998). Simon Reynolds writes of this disunity and fragmentation and shows why it is so difficult or even pointless to try and pin down any particular form of rave music as being authentic rave.

> Just as the Woodstock convergence gave way to the frag-
> mentation of seventies rock, just as punk split into
> factions based on disagreements about what punk was
> about and what was the way forward, so too has rave's
> E-sponsored unity inevitably refracted along class, race
> and regional lines. Each post-rave fragment seems to have
> preserved one aspect of rave culture at the expense of
> others. House music, in its more song-full, hands-in-
> the-air, handbag form, has reverted to mere disco, the
> soundtrack to trad Saturday Nite fever. Progressive house
> and garage is just your pre-rave metropolitan club land
> coked-out elitism back in full effect . . . Techno, ambient
> and electronica strip rave of its, well, ravyness . . . Jungle
> also incites a similar sense of urgency and zeal . . . You
> could call it 'Gangsta rave' . . . Music designed expressly
> for the E experience is still big . . . through the popularity
> of happy-hardcore . . . Scottish bouncy techno and

happy-core have preserved in miniature form the lost euphoria and togetherness of 1988–92 ... Happy hard-core is ... splitting up ... one element looks set to merge with Dutch gabba to form ... what some call 'fun-core' ... Jungle ... has of course already split up into at least three increasingly antagonistic subgenres.

(Reynolds 1998: 103)

Yet the potential to outrage 'rational' senses continues and forced the very public resignation of the British Vice-Consul of Ibiza as young people constructed a new 1998 'summer of love' just 10 years after the DJs Oakenfield, Rampling and Holloway put Ibiza on the map. The Ibiza phenomenon continues yearly to preoccupy both the British press and police. The British National Criminal Intelligence Service has in recent years been liaising with Spanish police units to try to bring an end to the hedonistic, drink and drugs summers much enjoyed by young British holidaymakers. In 1999, out of a total 900,000 visitors there were only 20 arrests for drug offences; this is something that seems not to worry the Spanish authorities but is seen as a case of 'bad policing' by the British. However, the attraction of Club Ibiza seems not to have waned as a wave of British clubs vie annually for the best venues. Manumission, Chic, UFO, Cream, Ministry of Sound, Freedom and Fusion are just some of the British clubs to set up their sounds in the summer of 1999 as Ibiza continued to award to clubbers the freedom to misbehave in a true 'carnival of rave' where the 'protest' comes from the carnivalesque. The media were once more fascinated with the sheer upfront hedonism of the young people concerned as if they, the media, had never experienced such consumer behaviour before. (I would have thought that just the sight of the opening day at a Harrods January sale would make most young people's consumer behaviour pale into insignificance.)

But rave in all its forms continues the post-modern theme of a fascination with sensation and the sensory mechanisms of the body. It is a quest for sensation without sense and without meaning. All life must be fun, immediate, ahistorical. The aim is to escape into sensation and stand free of logic. Rave culture becomes the perfect form of consumption without context or content, an apolitical and safe form of nothingness that challenges and shocks by its very concentration on the ecstatic out-of-mind experience that places the hedonism of the 'body' before the logic of the mind. 'Let the music take control' rather than 'real' life – 'Lifting me to the heavens in a state of ecstasy' into 'another time another place' (Newcombe 1992). This reminds us once more that 'the only real power of young people is to discomfort and to pose a threat' (Hebdige 1988). And so the body separates from the mind through the ecstatic use of both the physical activity of dance and the influence of 'E' and other drugs, leaving behind the trouble-laden world of modernity. Or as W. B. Yeats once asked,

> O body swayed to the music, O brightening glance,
> How can we know the dancer from the dance?
> ('Among School Children')

To be in a trance, to use Artaud's phrase, is to be 'doubled', not to be out of control or unconscious but simply to be possessed by another – like the character actor who acts out of character (Artaud 1958). To be in ecstasy is to be outside oneself, thus eliminating 'from the creative process the resistance and obstacles caused by one's own organism' (Gratowski 1968: 178). Both forms place the body in a relationship to both music and drugs that brings sense to what can be interpreted as senseless lives. The sensation is where the sense resides, making pleasure the site of meaning.

Music, dance, drugs and the individual body become reconciled within a form of rave culture that suggests that pleasure emanates from the body rather than the mind. For young people the body and its adornment become the primary site of defiance. You cannot after all be without a body. You can parade it in front of conservative society, flaunt it, dress it and pierce it, move it fast or slow or ultimately remove it altogether or be removed. You can make it predominant over the mind, or separate it altogether from the mind. You can perform with it, shock with it, play with it or abuse it. With music you can use the body to shock (as the gyrations of Elvis Presley excited a generation and shocked the parents of the 1950s) or you can put it in a trance with the rhythms of rave. In Brazil 'Funk Balls' combine body rhythm and violence as the 'ravers' fight to the music created by the 'mixer'. At hundreds of all-night raves, young people take the violence of the poverty in which they live and set it to music often fighting to the death, all controlled by the DJ.

The clubbing magazine *Ministry* demonstrated in its July 1999 'Body' issue this centrality of possessing your body through the culture of music. In that issue Tony Mitchel of the fetish magazine *Skin Two* talked of the coming together of clubbing and S&M. There were also features containing information on branding, scarification, piercing and body surgery, amongst other 'bodily alterations'. Club culture has emerged as a techno-culture that blends together the world of synthesised mixed music, technology, the body, cyberspace and sexuality into a truly post-modern cultural form (see Plate 7). Its very irrationality and emotionality bring it to the attention of the State and adult authority, who seek to control and watch over the body of its subjects that will make up the rational and ordered society of the future. The body, through music, becomes as a result a site of carnival for young people and hence a prime target for the criminalising process.

Drug laws are an example of this continuing criminalising of the body that is primarily aimed at young people. It is a process that even the police occasionally see as both futile and destructive. Detective Chief Inspector Ray Clarke, a former member of the Greater Manchester Police drugs squad, was reported in the *Independent* (29/9/97) as saying he was tired of the continuing criminalisation of 'otherwise innocent young kids' for using cannabis. At the same time the connection between drugs and dance has become more obvious and underlined by the number of reported deaths in 'club land'. This was further highlighted by the 1997 survey undertaken by the drugs agency Release, who after a survey of 520

Plate 7 Typical Seduction Company all weekender flier, October 1999

regular 'clubbers' found that 9 out of 10 took some form of drug whilst clubbing. But after a number of high-profile cases (such as the death of Leah Betts and the collapse of Helen Cousins on New Year's Eve 1995), it became clear that these cases were more to do with the necessity to take water as an antidote to the combination of dancing and drugs rather than the direct influence of 'E'. In a sense it was death by dancing rather than death by drugs. But Ecstasy quickly became a class A drug and was soon seen as the *bête noire* of club life. Yet the more open general discussion of the use of drugs in the 1990s ran counter to the Labour government's positioning of drugs as a major barrier to the road to 'work' and civilised life, which prompted their appointment of a 'Drugs Tsar' to lead the fight against drugs. Journalists wrote openly, admitting to using 'E'. After the death of Leah Betts, 19-year-old Libby Brooks wrote for the *Sunday Telegraph*, 'I am not a regular user but from time to time I like to get off my head'. This was a statement that Tom Hodgkinson agreed with when he acknowledged it as 'a trait she shares with this correspondent' (*Guardian* 16/11/96). Now even the Police Federation in its latest report on drugs is suggesting that Ecstasy should be downgraded from a class A to class C drug, thereby altering the legal vunerability of the half million club users every weekend (*Guardian* 17/2/00).

The consuming of 'E' as part of the culture of rave and clubbing led to the imprisonment of those who supplied the drug to their friends. As in most cultures that have as an integral part of their culture specific mind-altering substances, somebody has to get the goods, be it a six-pack, some fags, a strip of something, a packet, or some 'E'. In a cultural sense it feels no more different than sending out for a pizza. After the jailing of Joanna Maplethorpe for 9 months for getting the 'E' in for her friends, the *Sunday Independent* editorial wrote:

> Last night a million young people, maybe more, took ecstasy and Joanne Maplethorpe began a 9 month jail

sentence for supplying her best friend with an ecstasy tablet. Joanne Maplethorpe is not a pusher. Nor is your daughter or son.

(July 1997)

On the danger of Ecstasy, the Swiss Supreme Court ruled in June 1999 that it didn't pose a threat to either physical or mental health and as such was close to a 'soft' drug and that it saw no evidence to show that it led to criminal behaviour (*The Times* 16/6/99). The Court suggested that there are different views concerning the taking of such a cultural drug. But what is clear is that Ecstasy cannot be properly separated from a culture where the sensitised mind blending with the music is what is important to those who take part. As criminologist Mike Collinson so aptly pointed out,

> The world for young people is exciting, immediate, riskful and tempting and in the case of drugs consumption is orchestrated not by any value purpose or, at the other extreme, despair, nor by any explicit liberational project but merely to have a good time.
>
> (Collinson 1994: 4)

At the same time research undertaken at the Wembley Arena 1997 New Year's Eve Party clearly demonstrated that no matter what extent authorities go to in order to prevent drug-taking at rave parties, they will do little to halt the 'good time' rolling on. At this event 200 staff were employed for the following checks:

1) Ticket holders were checked to ensure they were 18 plus.
2) No one under the influence of alcohol or drugs was admitted.
3) Ticket holders were directed to 50 search lines where they were required to empty their pockets and remove their shoes and socks before being subjected to a full body search.

4) Coats and bags were also searched.
5) Performers were also searched as well as their bags and equipment.
6) Security guards confiscated and destroyed 23 types of drugs including Ecstasy and amphetamines.
7) Anyone claiming to be using prescription drugs was sent to a doctor for verification of their story.
8) Security guards confiscated chewing gum, Vicks vapo-rube and nasal inhalers.

The result of all this security was an average busy night where 79 collapsed cases were dealt with, 34 of which were clearly attributed to the use of Ecstasy, amphetamines, cocaine and Pro-plus concentrated caffeine (*Journal of Pre-Hospital Immediate Cure*, March 1999). However club managers are still attempting to provide help when needed and the Liverpool club Cream has now introduced the first in-house casualty support unit (*The Times* 27/11/99).

The regulation and criminalisation of club life continue as thousands of 'clubbers' who queue every night of the week, often late into the night, are continually harassed by the police and thereby exposed to the criminalisation process in practice. For example, the gay club Trade had its nine-year residency at the London club terminated in May 1999 after police raided its queue and arrested eight people. Moreover, later in June 1999 20 people were arrested both inside and outside the party held at the closed premises of the Hacienda (home of rave) club in Manchester which had been set up by a group affiliated to the Reclaim the Streets organisation. Seventy police were called to close the party and clear the queues outside.

But it was the 1994 Criminal Justice and Public Order Act introduced by the Conservative government that pushed the criminalising and regulation of youth to new levels, a process now supported and continued by the New Labour government of Tony Blair. The *Independent* newspaper commented on the Act:

15,171 clauses end the historic right to silence, [the Act] tackles such diverse issues as terrorism, prison privatisation, DNA testing, bail bandits, child offenders, and human embryo research, gives police greater stop and search powers and stamps on raves, squatting and mass protest.

(Independent 4/11/94)

But the Act's 'public face' was turned to the 'problem of youth'. The chairman of the Metropolitan Police federation described the public order provisions of the Act as 'unfathomable' and went on to say:

It appears to be legislation against a certain section of the population and that is a recipe for disaster. The whole aim of policing is to alienate the criminal – not to make criminals of people. Why are we legislating against people whose lifestyle, culture and attitude to life differ from other people?

(Independent 4/11/94)

The then Home Secretary Michael Howard made it clear who he was aiming at by clearly describing the behaviour he wanted to 'outlaw' when he made statements such as: 'Why should the selfish few be allowed to play music at intolerable levels late at night?' or 'We are not banning raves – properly organised and licensed events will not be affected' and 'We are also determined to deal with those who travel . . . en masse . . .' *(Independent* 19/10/94). Later he claimed that 'New powers will be at [police] disposal for dealing with public order such as raves, gatherings of new age travellers and mass trespass' (McKay 1996: 161). His public statements showed clearly his 'fear' of youthful behaviour and total ignorance of youth culture in all its forms. This fear and ignorance were perpetuated by the successive Labour government, whose own Public Disorder Act continues the process of the criminalisation of the young.

The 1994 Act fantasises about the life style of the young as its powers in relation to raves attempt to regulate the carnival of rave:

> This section applies to a gathering on land in the open air of 100 or more persons (whether or not trespassers) at which amplified music is played during the night (with or without intermissions) and is such as by means of its loudness and duration and the time at which it is played, is likely to cause serious distress to the inhabitants of the locality
>
> (sect. 62)

The ambiguity of the Act and its obsession with numbers then reduces the number that constitutes a rave from 100 to a situation where:

a) two or more persons are making preparations for the holding there of a gathering to which this section applies.
b) ten or more persons are waiting for such a gathering to begin there
OR
c) ten or more persons are attending such a gathering which is in progress.

(sect. 63)

The Act continues to state 'you may not go within 5 miles of a rave' (sect. 65) thus giving the police powers to stop all young people in a particular vicinity by virtue of their age and dress. How else would the police know who was or wasn't going to a nearby rave? It is little wonder that young people enjoy the warmth of the annual Iberian carnival as against the puritanical Cromwellian coldness of New Labour rationalism.

The anti-protest sections of the 1994 Act brought a new repression to the act of protest. Now two or more people gathering to protest is illegal (sect. 69), while it is possible for any assembly of 70 or more, even with limited rights of access, to be banned (sect. 70). At the same time violence against 'youth' became legally permissible when section 72 of the Act suspended section 6 of the Criminal Law Act 1977, thereby making it possible to use force in the eviction of squatters (who tend to be young people). At the time of the introduction of the Criminal Justice and Public Order Act the resistance by young people was considerable (McKay 1996) but to no avail, yet research undertaken by the Home Office to ascertain the effectiveness of this legislation concluded that it had had little effect on the social behaviour of young people and had achieved little except the strengthening of the legal position of the police. It reported one police officer talking about the 1995 Mother of All Raves as saying, 'You've just got to contain it and keep the locals happy' and on the policing of travellers, 'They moved on but they just moved to the other side of the street'.

Regrettably, the behaviour of young people continues to be feared and rigorously repressed, as in the baton charge exercised by 100 police in riot gear and using CS gas against those at an illegal rave at Summercourt near St Austell, Cornwall in August 1999, where the sound system was taken by the police like a war trophy. There can be little doubt that this was a 'battle' planned and executed along military lines, which in the end achieved little other than to reinforce the 'rightness' of the criminalising crusade against youth. This crusade surfaces once more the authorities' 'concern' over the music and culture of the displaced and diaspora as in rap and hip-hop.

In hip-hop and rap there is no need for special legislation to control and criminalise both music and culture, since the way of life that is 'talked' of, that makes up the story of the lives of the performers in a musical and rhythmic form, is already criminalised. Indeed what better way of saying the unsayable, of stating the illegal in a legal form, than bringing the re-actions of those in poverty and those from minority groups forward through the carnivalesque qualities of hip-hop and rap. As Redhead has pointed out,

> A hedonism in hard times is perhaps the best way to describe a sea of youth styles circulating in a harsh

economic and political climate where youth is increasingly seen as a source of fear for employed, respectable
society and a law and order problem for the police.

(Redhead 1993: 4)

It is the political and economic realities of life outside of
'polite' society that are reflected in rap as it analyses and celebrates the 'otherness' of poverty and struggle. It celebrates the
cultural 'answer' to ascribed social position and economic
survival, which includes the legal and illegal acquisition of
wealth, the struggle not just for work but the struggle at
work. It reflects oppression both through education and
through policing and the struggle for 'respect' in life. It not
only emphasises suffering but is also a celebration of leisure
time as the time free from the industrial processes of production (Gilroy 1987). And it is in the 'street' where others
daren't go that hip-hop and rap culture is lived and comes to
life. The aim is to be 'street-wise', to survive with 'dignity' and
'respect' amongst your own, without 'selling out'.

In the roll-call of rap stars, their names and song titles
reflect not only their clashes with the law but also the violence
involved in living a life of struggle and the maleness of the
culture, although female rappers and DJs have large follow-
ings as well and reflect their own struggle for survival. To give
some examples, there was the shooting of Tupac Shakur in
Las Vegas in September 1996 followed by Biggie Smalls
(Notorious B.I.G.), shot at the age of 24 in a rap war on
8 March 1997 not long after his last album *Life after Death*
and its ironic track 'You're Nobody Til Somebody Kills You'.
Ninjaman was imprisoned in Jamaica charged with murder,
reflecting his raps 'Murder Dem' and 'Murder Weapon'.
France's best-known rappers, Kool Shen and Joey Starr, were
jailed in 1996 for 6 months for anti-police lyrics 'Piss on the
brainless police machine' from the *Nique ta Mère* ('Fuck your
Mother') concert. Then Frankie Tah of the Lost Boyz was
shot dead on 29 March 1999. In April 1999 Sean 'Puffy'
Combs was arrested for beating up an employee of Interscope
Records and later also arrested for the possession of weapons.

Even BBC white rap DJ Tim Westwood was caught up in the struggle of the streets and was wounded in a street shooting in London in 1999.

The violence demonstrates the closeness that the stars of rap and hip-hop have with the community that they come from. They are in a sense still part of that struggle for both survival and the maintenance of whatever success they have achieved. It is a precarious position for all young people from these communities where 'nothingness' waits just round the corner, where acceptance and success are transient and culturally ephemeral, disappearing as quickly as they arrive. Along with clubbing and rave, rap completes the criminalisation of youth styles and creative culture that ensures that the continuing carnivalisation of everyday life will remain the major experience of being young.

8 The carnival and the performing of crime

Young people, knives and other weapons

There has been during the last five years throughout Europe and other Western states a classic 'moral panic' concerning the perceived decline of personal behaviour, which has heralded a lengthy public discussion on the relationship between morality and the motivation for social and economic life. This heightened concern has been brought about by a series of events from the Dunblane tragedy in Scotland to the murder of a London headmaster outside his school and, more recently, the Colorado school killings in the United States. The earlier events were ruthlessly appropriated by all the main British political parties during their autumn conference season and used, in the run-up to the last General Election, as their *raison d'être* for introducing further law and order measures and more regulations to be held over and against young people and their families. This has continued throughout the present Labour government's period of office and, not unsurprisingly, the debate about 'adult life' was jettisoned when it was realised that once again the real culprits were working-class young people and their families, who it appears have lost their civilised sense of right and wrong. New youth prisons, zero tolerance policing, and changes in the school curriculum along with the criminalisation of bad parenting are all aimed at the re-civilising of the poor and especially poor youth.

It is interesting that in the wake of the Colorado school shooting tragedy the American Congress has sought to criminalise both Goth subcultural forms and popular music lyrics (see Ch. 8) whilst the Louisiana state legislature has recently passed a Bill ensuring young people 'respect' their 'elders'. The Colorado tragedy was seen as directly contributing to the 'widespread support of the Bill' that was passed in Louisiana (*The Times* 8/7/99), aimed as always at young people. Meanwhile attempts after the Colorado tragedy by President Clinton to strengthen gun control laws, aimed at adults, failed once again.

In Britain the response to much violence came in the form of restrictions, not only on the ownership of guns but also on the selling to young people of any sharp object that could be construed as a weapon, such as scissors or art equipment. So the interpretation of the 1996 Weapons Act (sect. 6) and the Criminal Justice Act 1988 (sect. 141a) has meant that the selling of much kitchen equipment is restricted to adults alone. Sainsbury supermarket staff are now instructed not to sell sewing kits to young people under the age of 16, whilst Debenham's kitchen department in Cheltenham has stickers on much of its equipment and cutlery banning its sale to minors; even dessert spoons fall into the category of dangerous weapons. As I shall discuss in this chapter, this shows a complete misunderstanding of both the behaviour of young people and the social processes involved in the use of weapons.

At the same time a number of 'reports' described yet again the ever-widening wealth gap that exists alongside ever-increasing restrictions and regulations over social and economic life. These then are the individual and social conditions that make for the suppression of life that has in turn produced an ever-growing passion for destruction which in past times, would have been expressed in the revelry, riot and rebellion of the carnival (Fromm 1960: 158; Davies 1991; see also Ch. 3).

Control, carnival and crime

In a highly organised and controlled society based on the managed production and consumption of commodities, the State also takes significant control over the production of symbolic action and 'participatory pleasures'. This effectively removes from the activities of everyday life the ability to create meaningful and participatory acts which could function as resistance yet unify the collective. Unlike the world of carnival that Bakhtin (1984) describes, contemporary Britain is characterised by a network of imposed legal and moral constraints whereby the ability to create popular and meaningful carnival exists only in a superficial sense, being ever more tightly constrained and regulated by the Public Order Acts, as even dance clubs and 'parties' are closed down or licensed. Carnival, for Bakhtin, is a time when those silenced within the discourse of power can speak up. However, when the State regulates and licenses our symbolic and recreational life, then the spirit of carnival – the 'second life' of the people, as I have discussed previously – fragments, penetrating all aspects of social life. It is now harder and harder to be 'unofficial' and escape the rules, regimentation and regulations of the rational, legal world; thus the unofficial second life of the people is driven deeper and deeper from both view and comprehension. As Pettitt has pointed out, carnival has always contained the potential to 'detach itself from its specific seasonal context and acquire a function in revolt or unrest at other times, triggered by other factors' (Pettitt 1984).

The resulting debris contains all the characteristics of carnival, uncontained and unrestrained by the previously recognised restrictions of time and place and accompanied by the absence of the 'fool' who in the past continued carnival outside of carnival time, thereby adding to the fragmentation process and creating seemingly irrational and senseless acts that appeared not to fit any of 'life's available categories' (Docker 1996). Young people have often acted out the disruption of the clown at school and in the streets, resisting and rupturing the social fabric around them. Laughter destroys both science and rationality and is the precursor to freedom and truth. Bakhtin described well the power of humour so often used by young people in their predominant site of carnival, the school.

> Laughter . . . knows no inhibitions, no limitations . . . It was the victory of laughter over fear that most impressed medieval man. It was not only a victory over mystic terror of God, but also a victory over the awe inspired by the forces of nature, and most of all over the oppression and guilt related to all that was consecrated and forbidden . . . It was the defeat of divine and human power, of authoritarian commandments and prohibitions, of death and punishment after death, hell and all that is more terrifying than the earth itself. Through this victory laughter clarified man's consciousness and gave him a new outlook on life. This truth was ephemeral; it was followed by the fears and oppressions of everyday life, but from these brief moments another unofficial truth emerged, truth about the world and man which prepared the new Renaissance consciousness.
>
> (Bakhtin 1984: 90)

Civilisation and the forces of rationality attempt to criminalise the grotesque humour of the carnival, reducing laughter to mere giggles and a chuckling of the soul rather than the revolution and resistance of carnival humour. The seriousness of science is no laughing matter as all language becomes closed under the constraints of rationality. But carnival humour erupts in the second life of the people, the second State, where in a fragmented form it is pushed into the realm of the private and the individual, laughing at senseless authority and restriction from under the bedclothes or indeed in the toilet itself. Here, through the use of graffiti, we can laugh and shit at the same time, enjoying our own fragment of carnival to give us hope and strength for the world beyond. In 'official' life only equals may laugh, whilst the mere act of 'inferiors' laughing in front of 'superiors' destroys the false construction of respect. This is something that all young people quickly learn as they thread their way through the humourless world of modernity and its systems of education.

The following description shows well the lost dynamic of the clown and the potential for humour to continue carnival in the site of the school.

> I quickly learned I had little to offer. Instead I settled comfortably into the role of rebellious clown, perfecting, over time, the art of the quick quip and goonish behaviour. It was something that I was good at and enjoyed, being able to make the whole class laugh and sometimes even the teachers. It was as if I had control over them, just for that moment, making me the centre of attention; in control, shaping what happened. I knew when I had them 'with me', giggling along, trapped in the humour, wrecking people's defences or their attacks. Teachers would try and fight back smiles, but when the edge of their mouth went up, I knew I had them, and their power, just for a split second, left them, before they regained their composure and carried on.
>
> (Presdee 1988)

In this modern fragmented form a state of continual carnival exists, genuinely disrupting and shocking at an unprecedented level and intensity and thereby creating a social world of disruption all around (Docker 1996). As carnival fragments so do its inherent characteristics of excess, perversity, violence, riot, rebellion and revelry, which become continually acted out in dark streets. Here performers and audience merge into one whilst the reintegration function of carnival, its characteristic of reconciliation, is lost. What we now have in much social behaviour is all the transgression and violence of carnival isolated from the unifying process traditionally incorporated within it. Here carnival which previously resisted the 'pious' now challenges the 'industrious' with all its inherent contradictions. This shift from the original challenge to the restrictions of religion to a new resistance directed at the dominant meanings contained within a consumer society, where we are defined not by what we own but by what we consume, has created a culture of disruption, dissent and crime throughout everyday life.

Under these conditions carnival and crime merge into one and share the notion of liminality, that is the suspension of reality, being both out of place and out of consciousness. Now the carnival of crime, in contrast to the perfection of dominant forms of art and bodily beauty, has its own disruptive grotesque vocabulary of actions in the theatre of the fart, belch, vomit and defecation that is the very stuff of student rags and much 'new' comedy. It is the fragmentation of 'tops and bottoms' and the 'world upside-down'. Once more young people have claimed the grotesque of the carnival as their own domain, defying the restrictions and regulations of 'polite' society.

> I started to learn about violence as an answer to ridicule, and I started to glorify ugliness, learning how to disrupt the sensitivities of those from more sophisticated backgrounds. I learned who would be offended by a fart or a belch, by leaning on the wall, by a tie hanging down, by a cap not straight: I would show them what I thought of their sophistication, their manners, their world!
>
> (Presdee 1988)

The street and performance

The 'street' has long been a site of social performance and protest, and the place, *par excellence*, where carnival has become crime. As Edgar (1988) has shown, '[t]he site of carnival is in real space, in the actual social landscape, where the act of stepping off the pavement into the street transforms a spectator into a part of the action'. For young people the street has become the site for the celebration of riot, revelry and violent acts that, like carnival, are pregnant with excess and loyalty to the common community (communitas). In some sense there is a continuing struggle by young people to take possession of the street as their own space, whilst much policing is aimed at reclaiming what is perceived as public space. It is therefore no surprise to see young people defending the street, which often becomes the place where battle takes place.

Here the street becomes the setting and the stage where the drama of street action conveys the certainty of character (Goffman 1990) and where playing the role demanded of carnival affirms the behaviour of young people on the streets (Sartre 1957). Much of this behaviour, especially violent behaviour, is a 'cohesive and coherent drama, acted for an audience of friends, family and foe' (Armstrong 1994). Young people perform being tough in order to become tough, they dress for the performance of the fight and carry the costume of violence with them (Goffman 1990). But these performances emanate from the conditions in which young people find themselves, they cannot change roles to so-called better roles as if these were things in themselves. Meanwhile the execution of the performance itself, no matter how violent, produces all the passion and the pleasure of the theatre, without the safety of the vicarious experience that theatre allows for. Theatre is the containment of cathartic release; the carnival of crime is uncontained, real, lived, as in the sheer uncontained danger, drama and excitement of the improvised 'joyride'. The 'joyride' often ends in tragedy but like all improvisation it has a beginning and an end, yet is unscripted drama with no order to constrain plot or players. But as MacAloon (1984: 1, 9) has pointed out, there is always a 'risk that things might not go well. To agree to perform is to agree to take a chance'. Here within the violent drama of the streets is the 'deep play' of Geertz (1972) acted out like an improvised dance as evidence of exteriorised fantasy. Fantasy for many young people is the 'artificial dreams' of Adorno, which makes it possible to bear the rationality of official everyday life. The blocked displays of youth, their pent-up excitation and expectation, are frequently redirected inward where they are first transformed into fantasy then exteriorised as performance (Schechner 1988: 230). Young people now perform their lives (Turner 1985: 300) as their culture and social behaviour becomes theatre. In the same way that Schechner explains the high level of sex and violence in theatre as partially redirected activities, so too can the performance of sex and violent acts that are criminal also be explained in this way.

The performance of social, lived life can be examined as self-conscious or self-aware performance, that contains within it a range of levels of self-awareness. Certain performance moments seem to be naturalised, requiring no decision to perform on the part of the actor; for example, standard greetings or a telephone manner are performances that we fall into 'naturally'. Other activities are more self-aware, requiring as much mental and physical preparation as does the performance of an actor. Going out to fight is fraught with all the tension, fear and enjoyment of a full performance. For young people problems arise when certain self-aware performance acts become normalised and the drama of violence becomes a daily acting out of the carnival of crime.

> The real violence came later, when we were old enough to drink: then we would set out to invite violence, revel in it and, mixed with music, almost dance to it. It was then, later, that I lost bits of teeth and gathered scars and hit a few heads, getting barred and thrown out of shops, pubs, cinemas and dance halls.
>
> (Presdee 1988)

This characteristic of performance was described by Durkheim (1982) when connecting the notion of 'social effervescence' with the dramatic and violent performances of everyday life of the French Revolution.

On the Bonfire Night celebration night of 1999, before I set out to interview some young people, I observed performance in action when I came across a large group of young males around their bonfire set in the middle of an isolated space in the middle of a housing estate. I sat in the dark and watched them bouncing up and down in the middle of the fire on sprung mattresses placed over the fire. Like Fijian fire-dancers they danced and dared each other and dangled ropes into the heat of the flames, hurling them out and twirling the burning ends around their heads. Later they withdrew to the black corner of their green and watched the dying fire and listened to the background noise of staccato bursts of shell fire. Later they made bridges of burning boards that were placed over the fire and the dance began again as they began to joust and fight each other with burning sticks, the wind making the flames dangerous. Here was the performance of carnival contained by history, and yet this violent performance would, the next night, take on new connotations and become the carnival of crime.

Knives and weapons

The carrying of weapons, especially by young people, has exercised the minds of law-makers since the criminal code was developed. Stories, like the following, were common-place in the eighteenth century and illustrate how the idea of the unlawful possession of weapons was already established.

> 14 or 15 wild young fellows having provided themselves with clubs, swords, and other unlawful weapons, went about one o'clock in the morning to Neville's Alley in Fetter Lane, to pull down a house under pretence that a woman which they wanted was concealed there from them.
>
> (*Glos. Journal*, 3 Aug. 1731)

Later the 1824 Vagrancy Act allowed the police to arrest 'any person with any gun, pistol, hanger [dagger], cutlass or other offensive weapon . . . with intent to commit a felonious act'.

During the last knife amnesty in Britain, 40,000 weapons were handed in at police station. Under the new Offensive

Weapons Act 1996 it has become an offence to take weapons into schools and also to sell knives and other sharp objects to young people under 16 years. New proposals to stop and search those suspected of carrying knives is proposed by the present government, who are under pressure also to ban combat knives. However there has been little work done on whether knives are the first choice of weapon and whether such legislation will have any real effect on violence in the street. During this study I have interviewed a number of young men and women from North London, the North-east and the West of England about violence, weapons and the way that these are both created and used.

What becomes apparent is that it is the users of weapons themselves who define what a weapon is, through the very act of violence. And it is also clear that the violence many young people experience and create has become an important part of their everyday lives and a vital element in the formation of their identity. Weapons and the theatre of the street go hand in hand. Street fighting, especially with a weapon, becomes a performance unrestrained by the theatre itself, free of the constraints of script and the formality of discipline. It is deregulated drama.

There are distinct regional variations to the style of pre-ferred weapon. In London CS gas spray is the most popular: it has the potential to beat the biggest of enemies, is easily carried and easily obtained on daytrips to France (often bought during school excursions). It can also be bought at the local pub. One young person related, 'I have to admit me and me brother bought some gas at the pub for me mum. It only cost 20 and it's dangerous round here' (Gary). Planks, bricks and other articles 'to hand' such as beer glasses and bottles are popular throughout the country. There is no need to carry them and they can be disposed of quickly. In this way the objects of everyday life can soon quickly become a weapon.

> I was in this cafe and this guy came over and was making comments about me and me mate, and something about me mum. He thought he was being clever. I threw this

mug of hot tea over his face and walked out. I could hear him screaming from outside.

(Kev)

The most popular weapon throughout the country is a small baseball bat that can be concealed under a coat or in cars and is easily obtained from any sports store. Knives and other sharp objects are still being carried but they present more problems in transporting them, concealing them, and using them without getting into serious trouble. In the West of England, Pete explained,

> I had a knife . . . mainly for protection, like an army knife with a serrated edge, as well as an art and craft knife. . . . We used to have a baseball bat in the house in case anyone came to the house. We carried them all the time. . . . Dave always carried his knife and bat in the car and I carried mine with me. . . . That way we always had something with us.

This is confirmed by press reports, as below for an incident in 1996 in North London.

> Two boys aged 12 and 14 . . . were set upon by up to 18 youths aged between 13 and 17 who were carrying knives. The younger boy was hit over the head with a broken bottle while the older one was stabbed
>
> (*Guardian* 13/11/96)

Just before I interviewed one young man, I found out he had been involved in a street confrontation a few hours previously, and that it was still being investigated as we talked. He explained to me,

> One of them bottled one of the young Somali lads. I went up to them and said, 'Are you one of them?' and punched him in the face . . . You got to stick up for us . . . you got to stick up.

All this at 4.00 in the afternoon, involving no drink or drugs.

On the carrying of knives, lock knives were the most popular in London whilst larger meat cleavers or machetes proved popular elsewhere. Occasionally butterfly knives were carried because of the dramatic performance required to open them, which could impress the audience around you in the same way that cigarette lighters can be opened and lit using complex choreography. Various other cutting blades were carried, including Stanley knives and small art knives that could easily be concealed or, it was thought, easily explained away.

There was no doubt though that knives were being carried and that you 'tooled up if you're going to a wrong place or on a Sunday when it's boring'. A 'wrong place' could be defined as a trip to another neighbourhood, something you did especially when on a shopping trip that involved carrying large sums of money necessary to consume the style of say a 'Paul Smith' shirt, which was often the case. As in the case of female gang members in late nineteenth-century Manchester and Salford – scuttling gangs who had the important role of carrying weapons for male gang members and also perjured themselves in court to protect male members (Davies 1991: 72) – so young women nowadays seem often to play a part in the transportation of weapons. Pete explained that, 'If you've got a knife, you just give it to a girl but everyone carries something now'. Another group of young women told me that, 'If the police look as if they're going to stop us, us girls walk on in front and leave the boys behind to be searched. We act as if we don't know them'. This is borne out in another school-related incident that led to death from a stab wound. The prosecuting council said that 'it was commonplace for boys at the comprehensive school to be searched for knives but that girls were less likely to be subjected to searches' (*Telegraph* 5/7/96).

Other weapons were occasionally mentioned, but were not common. Pete talked of buying a 'stun gun off my mate for 70. I used it on me mate only having fun, you know. He fell to the floor and it frightened me so I took it to school and sold it for 90.' And Gary told of the time that even a car had been used.

There was a big fight the other Friday over drugs . . . They hadn't paid for them . . . One of them drove at us with their car and knocked one of us down. I was frightened. You can't use cars can you. We were all frightened.

School – the site where the State and adult society have the most effect and influence on young people's lives – and the streets that surround it, have become central to the violent carnival performances of young people. It is here that young people mystify authority with their own agenda, their activities considered unfathomable and grotesque by those in power.

School is where it all happens. My mate was handing out paper and it went on the floor. 'Pick it up,' he said. 'Fuck off, see you after school.' They all got together, it looked like the pied piper. They ruled and grouped up the next day.

(Kev)

Within a few weeks this confrontation, involving a number of groups, escalated into street warfare and an extravaganza of theatre.

They came down here and there were hundreds. Everywhere, they were everywhere. Cars loaded up. People everywhere. . . . I was frightened, I went home.

(Phil)

We were all picking up anything we could use. I'd never seen so many. In the end we kept out the way.

(Gary)

After several days a young man was stabbed and killed and new stories entered the folklore of the young people of the area. This memory without writing becomes part of the hidden history of an area. All the areas throughout Britain where we interviewed young people had their folk tales of murder and violence to be passed on to the next generation of youth, whilst graffiti highlighted the injustices suffered by those found guilty.

This telling of the story, the oral tradition, keeps alive the events for all concerned as they are elaborated on and refined over time. It also serves to keep alive hatred and conflicts, and ensures the process of resistance in the future.

> He [the gang leader] loves it, he thrives on it. It's like a show . . . He brags about what he's done. He loves telling people what he's done . . . It's like his party piece . . . He tells people . . . He loves it, it's a passion of his.
>
> (Gang member)

The young person found guilty of the murder of head teacher Philip Lawrence in London said in trial, when asked why he later told friends that he did it, 'I was boasting. It was the only thing that could make me look big' (*Guardian* 12/10/96)

Both these cases show an element of 'performing' by those involved, which was also an integral part of the acts they had performed already. In the case of the stabbing of Philip Lawrence, the element of performance was observable from the beginning. In this case the group dressed for the part, 'wearing bandannas, baggy trousers and loose jackets' (*The Times* 18/10/96) and then went on and 'met at Burger King . . . where they planned to descend on . . . the school. "One of the boys said it was going to be a laugh" the witness told the jury' (*Independent* 26/9/96). When the group marched on the school to take up an existing conflict, they marched in order of size and then when the performance went wrong, and confrontation occurred, their leader stabbed and killed the head teacher outside the school.

Here then is the drama of carnival deprived of its vicarious qualities. As young people 'play' the part they themselves have developed out of their material conditions, so they find that the violence of their performance is real and not imaginary. As Michael Bristol has pointed out,

The violence of festive misrule is not always symbolic, and whether symbolic or not, it is certainly not an incidental feature. If a theory of catharsis and reintegration is to account, even partially, for the overall shape of festivals such as carnival, it must be acknowledged that the transgressions associated with festival misrule are real and that, in the violence of festive misconduct real and sometimes irreparable damage will be done.

(Bristol 1985: 30)

And so it is for the debris of carnival.

To look for a separate knife or gun culture is to look for something that does not exist. Culture is a product, in part, of our reaction to the material conditions in which we find ourselves. It is the way that we make creative sense, rather than rational sense, of where we find ourselves within the labyrinth of social and economic structures that hang over and against us.

That is, culture is not in the subconscious, but rather, in modern language: it is value added. It comes on top of that with which we are presented. We make it in a myriad of ways, which is why it adds texture to our lives. It may not be 'moral' or 'right' or make sense to others but it is created by 'us' rather than by 'them', making the cocoon of culture an important space in which people, especially young people, can meaningfully live out their lives. It is therefore often impenetrable and alien to those 'outside' of these conditions. Yet in some fashion we are all 'outsiders', and it is those with power who in the end determine who will be designated 'outsiders', rather than anything particular in the way we live our everyday lives.

Many young people live out the drama of their lives within a general culture that has already commodified violence. They act it out on the stage of the street, performing with a passion the fragmentation of carnival. All the participants, performers and audience alike, play an important part in these sometimes violent activities, seduced by the desire for destruction and eager to become close to the excitement of combat and violence. Young men tell and retell their stories of violence that they have seen or been part of. Young women who profess to be non-violent are still active in the performances they watch.

> 'I don't like violence. I hate it.'
> ['Would you go out with a boy who was violent?']
> 'Well I expect my boyfriend to be hard. I'd want him to be hard, otherwise it wouldn't be any good going out with him. He couldn't protect you and that, look after you like. No I want him to be hard.'
>
> (Interview with Cathy)

Cathy talked of both the seduction and the repugnance of violence, and why she enjoyed her boyfriend.

> The danger . . . I know he can look after himself and he was exciting, you never knew what was going to happen next. Everyday is different. Fighting, music, drugs. The first night I went out with him he fought three bouncers. Afterwards I hated it, I collapsed. I couldn't handle it. But then I wanted more. I don't know.

Here destructiveness becomes the outcome of unlived life and in excitement the individual becomes both lost and found and may gain momentary relief from the burden of the constraints of inequality. It is this act of fragmented resistance, the anger within carnival (Fromm 1960), that constitutes the debris of carnival and which informs the everyday life of young people. It is here that the performance of violence will continue to leap from the liminal to life. The use of weapons is part of this particular cultural 'story' rather than, as in much of continental Europe, part of a culture of food, where knives are used in the everyday hunting, killing and production of food for the family. For example, the French have a habit not of attacking each other with oyster knives but of opening oysters with them! Knives in much of Europe are freely sold at all markets where weapons and knives of all shapes and sizes are

Plate 8 Typical French knife stall at a Saturday market (Photo by author)

displayed to be used in these social processes of everyday life. Not long ago I visited the live animal market at Samatan near Toulouse where there were literally thousands of live poultry for sale, not just for rearing but for the table. The French need and use knives for all occasions and for all jobs (see Plate 8). A culture of necessity frames the use whilst in England no such imperative exists, all that is left is the excitement of the conquest and the performance of violence.

> Holiday turned out to be an orgasm of music, fighting, drinking and fear. Every day was the same – breakfast followed by dancing, eating, dancing, drinking, sleeping, drinking, eating, dancing, fighting and sleeping. . . . We felt we were ordinary, one of the crowd; one of the masses.
>
> (Presdee 1988)

9   Senseless acts

The harbouring and harvest of hate

At the beginning of this book I began by talking of a number of seemingly senseless acts of violence during 1999 that had shocked populations throughout the Western world. During my writing there have been more mass killings as well as more military violence involving the forces of global authority, this time in East Timor. The political comments are the same; madness and evil seem once again to be the popular 'answers' accompanied by the production of the sort of 'panic' that sells papers. Yet again there has been a total lack of understanding of where the 'sense' in apparently 'senseless' acts comes from.

But it is not just violent acts that can be seen as senseless. Much crime, especially petty and social crime, is labelled in the same way: the coin or key dragged along the side of a car; tyres slashed; buildings defaced; schools burned; windows smashed. These are destructive acts that seem to have no rhyme nor reason, no meaning or sense. Crimes that have no monetary gain, such as joyriding, seem hard for us to understand and represent a behaviour with which scientific criminology finds it difficult to engage, being unable to categorise behaviour that appears alien in a society based on the acquisition of wealth. Rational choice theories of crime suggest that in a rational society we all, including criminals, think and behave in rational ways; all irrational acts stand outside of our comprehension and can only be designated as acts of evil or madness. 'You must be mad to steal a police car!' 'You must be mad to commit daylight robbery!' 'You must be evil to burn a school!' 'You must be mad to kill your family/ friends/lover!' Were serial killers Fred and Rosemary West mad or evil? The killer of head teacher Philip Lawrence mad or evil? Thomas Hamilton, who massacred the children of Dunblane, mad or evil? Or American Mark Barton, who killed both his family and fellow 'stock traders' after losing $205,000 on the stock markets, mad or evil? Yet weren't these acts seen as rational by the perpetrators as they attempted to explain them away in court or in the letters they left behind to explain their reasons for killing? The cry of 'evil' is both a measure of our collective shock and horror of the act itself and of our disbelief that our rational society could spawn such responses.

Yet violence, as I have tried to show, has become more of a way of life in this society. In the case of Fred and Rosemary West it was part of their everyday existence as they quietly went about their business of torture and violence. Sometimes violence is defined as an acceptable and rational response, whilst at others it is defined as unacceptable, irrational and senseless. The option to be 'violent', to use 'violence', to enjoy 'violence' and to watch 'violence', has become more of an acceptable behaviour and has permeated society. For example, new versions of martial arts seem to pop up every year and remain popular amongst both women and men. There are now nearly 2,000 female members of the Kickboxing Association in Britain alone. Indeed, the more actual bodily contact there is in such sports, the more attractive they appear to be. The coupling together of sex and violence is perhaps no more apparent than in the recent development of women's boxing, where the daughters of the once famous of boxing are now boxing regularly. This formula of fighting women, as in the spectacle of women mud-wrestling, has long been on the menu of the 'soft-porn' film-makers, but now it is becoming mainstream. The national research on violence being con- ducted at the time of writing shows that there are 5,000 'glassings' in pubs and clubs every year (ESRC 1998) and every time we are sold a drink in a plastic 'glass' we are, as a consequence, reminded that we are sitting in a site of violence.

But 'fun' and 'hate' seem to have merged together as the concept of 'hate' becomes an everyday recognisable concept. To hate and direct our hate outwards is also becoming more acceptable. In an age of popularised 'psychotherapy' we are told that to tolerate is wrong. We must let people know our true feelings and express our personal discontent through 'I' statements. 'I don't like how you look at me/how you eat/ what you wear/how you talk to me/how you sniff/cough/clear your throat.' The new therapies suggest that to tolerate is to become a victim of circumstances. We are told that what we need to do is express those feelings, thoughts, discontent and, in doing so, become a more complete person, an assertive person. We live in a culture where to express 'hate', to 'talk' hate, is increasingly encouraged because 'talk' is no longer communication but 'therapy' and good for us. The new mass site of hate is now the Internet, which runs thousands of 'hate pages' that sometimes openly admit to having 'fun' playing with hate and violence whilst others have an obviously more serious and violent intent (see Plates 9 and 10). But what they both want is for us to join in and share their hate. It is after all good 'therapy' for us and follows the methodology that offers therapy through both drama and art. We are urged to show our hate and tell people we hate them, as well as show what we would really like to do to them. Where these two sites I have chosen differ is that one appears acceptable, fun and 'understandable'; after all we all 'hate' the Spice Girls, don't we, so 'Death to the Spice Girls!' The other is deemed criminal and senseless.

One of the by-products of popular psychotherapies has become the production and acceptance of hate in everyday life which has become, like carnival, a site of licensed transgression. Where the popular therapists are mistaken is that, again like carnival, the hate that is expressed is not overcome and dissipated but is real hate that can be expressed time and time again. Therapy is no more than an individual carnival of the mind. One example is the prosecution of Richard

Plate 9 Racist hate site posted on Altavista

death to the Spice girls

"Hello! We're the Spice Girls. We really are completely natural, and even if we weren't famous *giggle* we'd all still dress like this. And put our make-up on with a spatula. There's nothing contrived about us at all....Nosiree, nothing at all.. Oh and before I forget. Girl Power! Yay! Oh no, I think my breasts are about to fall out..Oh well!"

For all those who are looking for Spice Girl sites, you've managed to do that quite successfully. Although, the same blithering idiots may not have realised that this is dedicated to the eradication of the Spice Girls and their evil influence on the world as we know it. If you're going to be mortally offended by it, go play your "Wannabe" single or something.

I mean this. The same goes to those righteous, pious people who are no doubt already forming "If you hate them so much, why do you waste your time on making a hate page" email in their heads. Go away. I don't want your type around here either.

Plate 10 Just one of the many Spice Girls hate sites posted on Altavista

Machado in the USA who, when accused of sending 59 Asian students hate mail at the University of California, stated that he sent the messages 'in jest'. This case has begun to undermine the notion of 'it's fun to hate' as it continues its path through the courts. Meanwhile the US Congress defines hate

> a crime in which the defendant intentionally selects a victim, or in the case of a property crime, the property that is the object of the crime, because of the actual or perceived race, color, national origin, ethnicity, gender, disability, or sexual orientation of any person.
>
> (sect. 280003a, Violent Crime Control and Law Enforcement Act 1994)

The rise of hate crime has been closely monitored in the USA whilst in the United Kingdom evidence of crimes with a racial/hate element are only just beginning to be taken account of. The Simon Wiesenthal Center in Los Angeles suggests that there are over 400 race hate groups in the USA with well over 2,000 serious hate sites on the Internet. Meanwhile the US Criminal Justice Information Services department statistics on hate crime showed that in 1996 there were 11,039 violent hate crimes against the person and 3,669 offences against property. Given the difficulties in attempting to gather statistics about any category of crime let alone the motivations for it, the accuracy of these figures must be in doubt.

What cultural artefacts tell us is a story not only about the everyday native of violence but how it continues to be enjoyable, exciting and often acceptable and good fun. Fun with violence has now become an acceptable consumer commodity whether it is visual (as in many 'hate' pages) or real (as in much sport). In a recent interview in the *Independent* newspaper the ex-England rugby player, Martin Bayfield, described the sheer unashamed fun of violence involved in the sport of rugby that he felt able to share openly with hundreds of thousands of readers as he described his treatment of South African forward Johan le Roux.

Every time we went clattering into a ruck or maul we'd punch him and kick him and every time he'd be yelling 'I love it, I love it, give me more!' We thought 'what a nutter' . . . Also I remember piling into a ruck against New Zealand and everyone of us ran up Sean Fitzpatrick's back. We gave him a real hard going over.

(*Independent* 15/9/99)

Here there is a real delight in being both deviant and destructive as sport becomes the socially acceptable face of 'race hate' that we enjoy as part of a shared nationalism reproduced as a cultural commodity on television. Even pop videos such as 'Bitter Sweet Symphony' by The Verve consist of nothing more than street violence to strangers put to music.

But where does the 'hate' come from that produces such senseless acts? The problem arises from the inability of the system of rational liberalism to comprehend the failure of the quest for modernity to produce a scientific/rational blueprint for life to adequately explain why we suffer or not, endure poverty or not. We no longer accept that if we do not have this or that qualification, or if we achieve less in production than others, then we logically deserve less, should have less of the produced resources, should *be* less. We no longer accept that failure to succeed is our failure; instead we seek to put the blame somewhere else. In other words 'rational argument' no longer works, if indeed, it ever did, to position action on the right/wrong continuum. The ideological control mechanisms that 'explain' to us all why we live as we do, why we appear successful or not, which constitute the 'accepting' mechanisms of our society, appear to have failed. If there are perceived injustices in the everyday lives of people, then 'hate' is both produced, stored and dammed up behind the flimsy facade of rationality. Blame is the result.

For example, for all the so-called advances both social and legal, in divorce and separation processes, including the rational notion of 'no blame', the Anna Karenina factor is still with us. No matter how much rational/legal norms are held over people, hate as a result of emotional hurt continues to show itself in hateful acts of blame and bitterness which may easily continue for a lifetime, with hate being aimed at the individuals or groups that are seen, rightly or wrongly, as the source of hurt. These sources may be governments, institutions, employers, spouses, ex-spouses, managers, teachers or simply 'authority'. Hate comes from both loss and failure, the negative factors of life lived from within a competitive society where powerlessness for many is an everyday experience. The response is not necessarily personal violence but simply the search for sense in what appears to many to be a senseless world. Suicide is often just another such escape from the unbearable structures and strictures of modernity, so it's not surprising that 80 per cent of all suicides are males aged between 15 and 24 years.

We find certain acts senseless because to us the act is irrational, outside the meaning of scientific rationalism. It is senseless to us but not to the perpetrator of the senseless act. In a powerless world, crime creates power for the individual to express their individuality. The very aesthetics of crime resides in its irrationality. This is the art in crime rather than the art of crime and in turn creates crime's seductive nature.

Rational liberalism is hoist then on its own petard. Much crime and disorder are the wrong social/human response to living in a rational society. What rationality cannot accept is the rejection by its own subjects of the consequences of living rationally. Rationalism demands the acceptance of order as the object of the rational/scientific project of which liberalism is its political edge. Control is a necessary and rational exercise that in practical terms leads to the putting in place of the electronic panopticon that now surveilles our everyday lives. Control no longer resides just in institutions or at work but is all around us, checking whom we phone and when, what we spend and when, where we travel and when, how we play and when. We leave behind us a trail of electronic information that can be used for our own good to protect both ourselves and commerce from the outsiders.

As I have said elsewhere (Presdee 1990), the more an economy is deregulated, the more the subjects of such a society need to be surveilled and regulated. Such an approach, like bureaucracies, is both rational and efficient yet personally unbearable and the very font of crime. Weber's 'iron grip of instrumental rationality' suffocates the modern soul in contrast to the possibility of the creativity of both carnival and crime. Crime then becomes the 'risk' of rationality, a by-product of commodity production, and as such is a part of the waste of consumption alongside all the other waste products created by the production and consumption process. The 'enchantment' of consumption hides the 'disenchantment' of the production process, which demands that both production and consumption be controlled. As disenchantment with controlled consumption increases, so uncontrolled, irrational criminal consumption increases. Indeed, crime is uncontrolled consumption where criminals are fraudulent consumers but consumers nevertheless.

The explanation of 'evil' as the cause of crime shifts the debate neatly away from the questioning of rationality itself and its dynamic which 'propels efficiency and growth' and which 'is itself irrational' (Marcuse 1972: 12). The critique of the rational/scientific society tells us more about the causes of crime than the superstitious explanation of 'evil' proposed by those who drive the dynamics of efficiency. As the individual becomes more and more trapped by applied science and the rational, so we become more and more enmeshed and oppressed within the so-called scientific measurement of our lives. League tables and targets determine our actions as we live from inside the politically constructed matrices of life. Indeed, we no longer have 'lives' but instead 'outcomes' of rationally constructed policies. We become 'fixed', 'positioned' and 'placed' as society is no longer made up of human interaction but rather human sediment. Of course the measurements that trap us are in reality made-up measurements that in themselves prove that the rational way is right. The measurements prove that we are improving as human beings or not, that we are using resources efficiently or not, and that if we follow the formula as offered we will soon have the good life. Spontaneity is seen as part of the 'natural', and to be 'natural' is to be savage and not part of scientific rationality. As a result the irrationality that is the second spontaneous life of the people becomes a crime in itself, that is, to think irrationally, to behave irrationally, becomes in itself a crime and the resulting behaviour becomes quickly criminalised. In other words everyday life is subjected to a creeping criminalisation process where the carnival of crime becomes a central necessity in our lives.

Scientific rationality demands that we place rational choice first, whilst individual choice becomes a second-order consideration. Individual autonomy becomes an irrational act within a scientific society. As a replacement for autonomy we 'read' and recognise ourselves through the measurements made by others of our lives. It is life as 'league table'.

Yet modernity is in itself the most rational form of irrationality with its dominance of quantitative thought over qualitative thought. Its political forms, such as New Labour politics, become a self-validating process whereby measurements break down 'life' into more and more minute human skills so that there can be no escape from becoming perfect. We are now cluttered with the certificates of competency that tell us where we stand on the scale of humanness, whilst political debate becomes debased with discussions about measurements and methodology rather than about humanity.

In our everyday lives our individual identities become 'managed' and 'worked on' as the contradictions of character are identified and sent away to be smoothed out by the therapists of modernity. The transcendence of structure by the self can no longer be an option. If we are madly in love or obsessional we can be cured by the psychiatrist; conflict within the self appears to be resolved but is instead repressed. Under the apparent 'order' of modern managed life lie the chaos, anger and hate that erupt in criminal and deviant acts both confounding and confusing the project of modernity. In this new social order the 'disruptive characters such as the artist, the prostitute, the adulteress, the great criminal and outcast, the warrior, the rebel-poet, the devil, the fool – those who don't earn a living, at least not in an orderly and normal way' (Marcuse 1972: 59) – appear senseless, thankless, irrational and a threat to the future of society and are deemed either criminal or deviant or both. The policies of the New Labour government herald the new Dark Ages of scientific rationality. Their policies are in themselves defined as rational and responsible and open to all. Failure to take up the perfect policies on offer that will purportedly lead to social 'inclusion' is consequently defined as irresponsible and irrational. We are told that there is no longer any poverty, only those who choose to stand outside of society, who become not the 'excluded' (because exclusion no longer exists) but the 'outsiders' who inhabit the invisible and criminal fourth dimension of social life. As a result, for New Labour, all rational explanations for crime seem now to have been eradicated, enabling us once more to see clearly that the 'criminal classes' are no more than the 'undeserving poor'. The criminologists of New Labour have successfully reconstituted the 'underclass' of conservative politics as the 'undeserving poor' of New Labour, rather than recognising that their policies as such define 'wrong-doing' and create categories of crime rather than eradicate them. The Labour government's rational response to crime of imprisoning the criminal classes is in reality no more or less than the imprisonment of culture.

In reality, as I have tried to show throughout this book, it is the everyday response to structured life that is the spawning ground for so much of what we call crime. We have to realise that there are at the moment people in gaol in Britain for such diverse behaviours as: partying in the wrong place, speeding, roadrage, using a mobile phone on a plane, using a laptop computer on a plane, 'smacking' someone's bottom in the street, breaking a branch of an ancient tree, badger-baiting, organising dog-fights, arson, making music in the open, stalking, stealing dead bodies for art, hating, hacking and joyriding. The list goes on and becomes more and more extensive as we add all the social behaviours that people have been found guilty of but not imprisoned for, such as making love in your back garden and having sex on a plane, or 'pissing' in the street. What we must never forget is that the bulk of crime is created through the criminalisation and policing of social behaviour as against dishonest behaviour and that it is a crime to be many things including poor, young, disadvantaged, to fail and even at times to be creative.

I have tried here to widen and add new dimensions to the existing debate within criminology and to add human emotional texture to the social behaviours that we call criminal. In the end it is human beings, living within and responding to a web of social and economic structures, created through historical struggle, who 'do' crime. In the end too only a humanistic and therefore cultural criminology can do justice to the analysis of humankind and its hurts, injustices and expressions of individuality that are all part and parcel of crime.

What then is the future for criminology and specifically for cultural criminology? It is clear that the existing debates within criminology appear to have come to a halt, restricted by the very administrative rationality they sought to analyse. The analysis has become moribund; yet pockets of intellectual bravery exist, as in the writings on state crime, carrying with them some intellectual momentum, pushing at the boundaries of enquiry. Where administrative criminology fails is in its misunderstandings of the culture of everyday life and the importance for many of doing wrong and doing crime. Resistance through culture needs to be re-theorised and grasped once again. But also too the aesthetics of crime needs to become a central debate in criminology alongside the notions of pleasure, desire and consumption. Indeed, if pleasure and desire are essential ingredients in a super-controlled consumer society, then criminological enquiry needs to reflect this fact.

Cultural theory has the potential to unearth the aesthetics of the everyday and therefore cultural criminology has the potential to unearth the processes involved in the aesthetics of crime, unravelling the minutiae of cultural 'meaning-making' whereby social behaviour becomes criminal behaviour. But questioning the process of criminalisation is itself a dangerous activity and is likely to incur the wrath of those with the most power, who have the most to lose and therefore the most to protect. Much cultural criminology in its quest to privilege personal experience and emotions is itself an exercise in edgework with all the risks that brings. Opening up ourselves to be analysed by all seems a foolish enterprise but is a necessary part of the process of going forward. Putting others under the social microscope is in itself problematical and assumes that we know where the fault lies and administrative criminology knows instinctively it doesn't lie with us! For too long cultural theorising as against ethnographic description has been hidden in contemporary criminology. All the concerns of contemporary cultural studies need now to be brought to bear on the question of crime. This must encompass the question of consumption and the meaning of media; the creation of identity in a post-modern society and the use of biography and life histories; commodification and cultural artefacts; popular culture and everyday life; excitement, pleasure and desire; sexuality, gender and culture; fashion, fads, and fun. All have a place in the conceptual armoury of cultural criminology. There are of course pitfalls that await us, such as over-indulgence and overly 'romantic' interpretations, but I believe that the gains to our understanding of crime far outweigh the intellectual risks. In that sense we have a duty to those we study to take their claims seriously and to be as creative and sensitive as we can in the interpretations we make and the understandings we put forward. Cultural criminology studies the systems we create through an analysis of the everyday lives of people. Human emotional and material experience in all its richness and complexity is where we start; the economic and social systems that result are where we end.

As I got older so my life became more like a battlefield with the battle lines rigidly drawn up, as if preordained. I had no real answer to my feelings of injustice, other than defiance and violence, that they in turn countered with more aggression, in their attempts to control, contain and make ordered. In time I created, with my friends, a veneer of violence that, like the spikes of a porcupine, became part of us, an evolved defence mechanism that could be used, when all else failed, to attack and push back. Mainly we lived with our spikes just 'there', bristling, and daring anyone to touch us, or control us.

Yet it was all still confusing, because porcupines were useful in sport, especially in the front row of a rugby scrum, or armed with a hockey stick. Gradually our very defiance and violence were appropriated by the controllers, for their ends. They helped to make us: they held us, controlled us, then unleashed us in their service. From the estate we joined the armed forces, became policemen and prison warders, security guards and bouncers. We were ripe for the unleashing; working-class watchdogs turned out to snarl and keep in order the mass of the working classes, as we watched over the interests of the controllers. I was saved from delinquency by being delinquent for them, exercising my vice so they could be virtuous. I joined the Marines. Now I could be let loose on the enemy, their enemy, and be defiant, cunning and violent; a legal delinquent; and instead of fighting authority I would fight for it: or so they hoped. I became a State 'minder'.

The third service they provided for the estate was law and order. They built two police stations for us, either side of the green, like sentry boxes guarding the entrance to the estate. Now we would be able to sleep safely; know when we were breaking the law and become law-abiding, honest citizens. We would know when were doing wrong: we were nearly complete.

(Presdee 1988)

References

Adorno, Theodor (1984) *Aesthetic Theory*, London and New York: Routledge.

Anderson, Sean E. and Howard, Gregory J. (ed.) (1997) *Interrogating Popular Culture: Deviance, Justice, and Social Order*, Guilderland, NY: Harrow & Heston.

Armstrong, G. (1994) 'False Leeds: The Construction of Hooligan Confrontations', in Giulianotti, R. and Williams, J. (ed.) *Game without Frontiers*, Aldershot: Arena.

Armstrong, G. and Giulianotti, R. (1996) 'Law and the Football Hooligans' (unpublished paper).

Artaud, A. (1958) *The Theatre and Its Double*, London: Grove Press.

Bakhtin, Mikhail (1973) *Problems of Dostoevsky's Poetics*, Michigan: Ann Arbor Press.

Bakhtin, Mikhail (1984) *Rabelais and His World*, Bloomington: Indiana University Press.

Barak, Gregg (ed.) (1994) *Varieties of Criminology: Readings from a Dynamic Discipline*, Westport, Conn. and London: Praeger.

Baudrillard, Jean (1996) *The Perfect Crime*, London and New York: Verso.

Benjamin, Walter [1955] (1970) *Illuminations*, London: Fontana.

Benjamin, Walter (1973) *Baudelaire: A Lyric Poet in the Era of High Capitalism*, London: New Left Books.

Bennett, T. (1983) 'A Thousand and One Pleasures: Blackpool Pleasure Beach', in Formations Collective (ed.) *Formations of Pleasure*, London: Routledge & Kegan Paul, pp. 138–145.

Bourke, Joanna (1999) 'The Pleasures of War', J. Bourke, *An*

Intimate History of Killing: Face to Face Killing in Twentieth-Century Warfare, London: Granta Books, pp. 13–43.

Bouvier, J. M. (1994) 'Le carnival, la fête et la communication'. Paper presented at the conference 'Rencontres Internationales de Nice: sens et fonction de la fête', 1994.

Brain, D. (1979) *The Decorated Body*, London: Hutchinson.

Braithwaite, J. (1989) *Crime, Shame and Reintegration*, Cambridge: Cambridge University Press.

Brake, M. (1990) 'Changing Leisure and Cultural Patterns among British Youth', in L. Chisolm, P. Büchner, H.-H. Kruger and P. Brown (eds) *Childhood, Youth and Social Change*, London: Falmer.

Brame, Gloria G., Brake, William D. and Jacobs, Jon (1997) *Different Loving: The World of Sexual Dominance and Submission*, London: Arrow Books.

Braudel, Fernand (1985) *The Structures of Everyday Life*, London: Fontana Press.

Bristol, M. (1985) *Carnival and Theatre*, New York: Methuen.

Burgess, Anthony [1962] (1996) *A Clockwork Orange*, London: Penguin.

Burgess, Anthony (1991) *You've Had Your Time*, London and New York: Penguin.

Campbell, B. (1993) *Goliath: Britain's Dangerous Places*, London: Methuen.

Carlson, Marvin (1996) *Performance: A Critical Introduction*, London and New York: Routledge.

Cavani, L. (1977) 'Cinéma et érotisme', in Michèle Causse and Maryvonne Lapouge (eds) *Écrits, voix d'Italie*, Paris: Éditions de Femmes.

Chancer, Lynn S. (1992) *Sadomasochism in Everyday Life: The Dynamics of Power and Powerlessness*, New Brunswick and New Jersey: Rutgers University Press.

Cohen, Phil (1997) *Rethinking the Youth Question: Education, Labour and Cultural Studies*, London: Macmillan.

Collinson, Mike (1994) 'In Search of the High Life: Drugs, Crime and Respect'. Paper presented to the American Society of Criminology, Miami, November 1994.

Cook, K. (1994) 'Cradled in Punitiveness: Abortion Opponents, Death Penalty Supporters and the Politics of God's Will'. Paper presented to the American Society of Criminology annual conference, November 1994.

Curry, D. (1993) 'Decorating the Body Politic', *New Formations*, 19: 69–82.

Davies, A. (1991) 'Histories of Crime and Modernity', *British Journal of Criminology*, 39: 72–88.

Debord, Guy (1983) *Society of the Spectacle*, Detroit: Black & Red.

Debord, Guy (1990) *Comments on the Society of the Spectacle*, London and New York: Verso.

Deleuze, Gilles (1997) *Masochism: Coldness and Cruelty*, New York: Zone Books.

Demos (1999) *Destination Unknown*, London: Demos.

Dentith, Simon (1995) *Bakhtinian Thought: An Introductory Reader*, London and New York: Routledge.

Diamond, E. (ed.) (1996) *Perfomance and Cultural Politics*, London: Routledge.

Diamond, I. and Quinby, L. (eds) (1996) *Feminism and Foucault: Reflections on Resistance*, Boston: Northeastern University Press.

Docker, John (1996) *Postmodernism and Popular Culture: A Cultural History*, Cambridge: Cambridge University Press.

Douglas, Mary and Isherwood, Baron (1979) *The World of Goods: Towards an Anthropology of Consumption*, London and New York: Routledge.

Durkheim, E. (1982) *Formes élémentaires de la vie religieuse*, Paris: Éditions de Minuit.

Eco, Umberto, Ivanov, V. V. and Rector, Monica (1984) *Carnival*, The Hague: Manta.

Edgar, D. (1988) *The Second Time as Farce*, London: Lawrence & Wishart.

Elias, N. (1991) *The Symbol Theory*, London: Sage.

Elias, Norbert and Dunning, Eric (1993) *Quest For Excitement: Sport and Leisure in the Civilising Process*, Oxford: Blackwell.

Elliot, C. (1992) 'The Thin Blue Line between Arrest and Escape', *Young People Now*, 34.

Ellis, H. (1942) *Studies in the Psychology of Sex*, New York: Random House.

Ellul, Jacques (1992) *Déviances et déviants*, Toulouse: Eres.

Epstein, Jonathan S. (ed.) (1998) *Youth Culture: Identity in a Postmodern World*, Massachusetts: Blackwell.

ESRC (1998) *Taking Stock: What Do We Know About Violence?*, London: Economic and Social Research Council.

168   *References*

Featherstone, Mike (ed.) (1999) *Love and Eroticism*, London: Sage.

Fenwick, M. and Hayward, K. (2000) 'Youth Crime, Excitement and Consumer Culture', in J. Pickford (ed.) *Youth Criminal Justice Theory and Practice*, London: Cavendish.

Ferrell, Jeff (1996) *Crimes of Style: Urban Graffiti and the Politics of Criminality*, Boston: Northeastern University Press.

Ferrell, Jeff and Hamm, Mark (ed.) (1998) *Ethnography at the Edge: Crime, Deviance, and Field Research*, Boston: Northeastern University Press.

Ferrell, Jeff and Sanders, Clinton S. (1995) *Cultural Criminology*, Boston: Northeastern University Press.

Fishman, Mark and Cavender, Gray (1998*) Entertaining Crime: Television Reality Programs*, New York: Aldine De Gruyter.

Fiske, John (1991) *Understanding Popular Culture*, London and New York: Routledge.

Formations Collective (eds) (1983) *Formations of Pleasure*, London: Routledge & Kegan Paul.

Fornas, Johan, Lindberg, Ulf and Sernhede, Ove (1995) *In Garageland: Rock, Youth and Modernity*, London and New York: Routledge.

Foucault, M. (1977) *Discipline and Punish*, London: Allen Lane.

French Vocabulary Handbook (1994) ed. Kate Dobson, Oxford: Berlitz.

Freud, Sigmund (1955) *Civilisation and Its Discontents*, London: Hogarth.

Frisby, David (1992) *Simmel and Since: Essays on Georg Simmel's Social Theory*, London and New York: Routledge.

Frisby, David and Featherstone, Mike (1997) *Simmel on Culture*, London: Sage.

Frith, S. (1986) 'Art versus Technology: the Strange Case of Popular Music', *Media, Culture and Society*, VIII (3).

Fromm, Erich (1960) *Fear of Freedom*, London: Routledge & Kegan Paul.

Fromm, Erich (1976) *To Have or To Be?* New York: Harper & Row.

Fyvel, T. R. (1961) *The Insecure Offender*, London: Chatto & Windus.

Game, Ann and Metcalfe, Andrew (1996) *Passionate Sociology*, London: Sage.

Gates, Henry Louis, Jr (1995) 'Sudden Def', *The New Yorker*, 19 June.

Geertz, Clifford (1972) 'Deep Play: Notes on the Balinese Cock-fight', *Daedalus*, 101: 1–37.

Gilroy, C. (1987) *There Ain't No Black in the Union Jack*, London: Hutchinson.

Goffman, Erving (1963) *Behaviour in Public Places: Notes on the Social Organisation of Gatherings*, Glencoe, Ill.: Free Press.

Goffman, Erving (1990) *The Presentation of Self in Everyday Life*, London: Penguin.

Gouldsblom, J. and Mennell, S. (eds) (1998) *The Norbert Elias Reader*, Oxford: Blackwell.

Grabosky, P. N. and Smith, Russell G. (1998) *Crime in the Digital Age: Controlling Telecommunications and Cyberspace Illegalities*, Leichhardt Australia: Federation Press.

Gratowski, J. (1968) *Towards a Poor Theatre*, Holstebro, Denmark: Odin Teatrets Forlag.

Groombridge, Nic (1998a) ' "Car Culture": Advertising, Joyriding and Gender'. Unpublished paper.

Groombridge, Nic (1998b) 'Masculinities and Crimes against the Environment', *Theoretical Criminology*, 2 (2): 249–267.

Grosz, Elizabeth and Probyn, Elspeth (eds) (1995) *Sexy Bodies: The Strange Carnalities of Feminism*, London and New York: Routledge.

Hamm, Mark S. (1994) *American Skinheads: The Criminology and Control of Hate Crime*, Westport, Conn. and London: Praeger Press.

Hardy, Simon (1998) *The Reader, the Author, His Woman and Her Lover: Soft-core Pornography and Heterosexual Men*, London and Washington: Cassell.

Harris, David (1992) *From Class Struggle to the Politics of Pleasure: The Effects of Gramscianism on Cultural Studies*, London and New York: Routledge.

Hartley, J. (1994) 'Twoccing and Joyriding', *Textual Practice*, 8: 3.

Harvey, David (1989) *The Conditions of Postmodernity*, Oxford: Blackwell.

Hebdige, D. (1988) *Hiding in the Light: On Images and Things*, London and New York: Routledge.

Hill, Christopher (1991) *The World Turned Upside Down*, London: Penguin.

Holquist, Michael (1984) 'Prologue' in Bakhtin, M., *Rabelais and His World*, Bloomington: Indiana University Press.

Hunt, Leon (1998) *British Low Culture: From Safari Suits to Sexploitation*, London and New York: Routledge.

Jameson, Fredric (1991) *Postmodernism: Or the Cultural Logic of Late Capitalism*, London and New York: Verso.

Jeanmaire, H. (1951) *Dionysos: Histoire du culte de Bacchus*, Paris: Payot.

Jervis, John (1999) *Transgressing the Modern*, Oxford: Blackwell.

Josephson, Mary and Josephson, Eric (eds) (1972) *Man Alone: Alienation in Modern Society*, New York: Dell.

Kappeler, Susanne (1995) *The Will to Violence: The Politics of Personal Behaviour*, Cambridge: Polity Press.

Katz, Jack (1988) *Seductions of Crime: Moral and Sensual Attractions in Doing Evil*, New York: Basic Books.

Kershaw, B. (1992) *The Politics of Performance*, London and New York: Routledge.

Klausner, Samuel Z. (ed.) (1968) *Why Man Takes Chances: Studies in Stress-seeking*, New York: Anchor Books.

Krafft-Ebing, R. von (1947) *Psychopathia Sexualis: A Medico-Forensic Study*, New York: Pioneer.

Lasch, C. (1979) *The Culture of Narcissism*, London: Abacus.

Lefebvre, Henri (1971) *Everyday Life in the Modern World*, New York and London: Harper Torchbooks.

Lefebvre, Henri (1976) *The Survival of Capitalism*, London: Alison & Busby.

Levine, Donald N. (1971) *Georg Simmel on Individuality and Social Forms*, Chicago: Chicago University Press.

Louis, Patrick and Prinaz, Laurent (1990) *Skinheads, Taggers, Zulus and Co*, Paris: La Table Ronde.

Lyng, S. (1990) 'Edgework: A Social Psychological Analysis of Voluntary Risk Taking', *American Journal of Sociology*, 95: 887–921.

Lyng, S. (1998) 'Dangerous Methods: Risk Taking and the Research Process', in J. Ferrell and M. S. Hamm (eds) *Ethnography at the Edge: Crime, Deviance and Field Research*, Boston: Northeastern Press.

MacAloon, J. J. (ed.) (1984) *Drama, Festival, Spectacle: Rehearsals towards a Theory of Cultural Performance*, Philadelphia: Institute for the Study of Human Issues.

McClintock, A. (1993) 'Maid to Order: Commercial S/M and Gender Power', in Pamela Church Gibson and Roma Gibson (eds) *Dirty Looks: Women, Pornography, Power*, London: BFI.

McCracken, Grant (1990) *Culture and Consumption*, Bloomington: Indiana University Press.

McKay, George (1996) *Senseless Acts of Beauty: Cultures of Resistance Since the Sixties*, London and New York: Verso.

McKay, George (1998) *DIY Culture: Party and Protest in Nineties Britain*, London and New York: Verso.

MacKay, Hugh (ed.) (1997) *Consumption and Everyday Life*, London: Sage.

McRobbie, Angela (1994) *Postmodernism and Popular Culture*, London and New York: Routledge.

Malbon, Ben (1999) 'Clubbing: Consumption, Identity and the Spatial Practices of Every-night Life', in T. Skelton and G. Valentine (eds) *Cool Places: Geographics of Youth Cultures*, London: Routledge.

Marcuse, Herbert (1972) *One Dimensional Man*, London: Abacus.

Martin, P. J. (1995) *Sounds and Society*, Manchester: Manchester University Press.

Marx, Karl (1977) *Karl Marx: Selected Writings*, ed. D. McLelland, Oxford: Oxford University Press.

Mestrovic, Stjepan G. (1997) *Postemotional Society*, London: Sage.

Miller, Philip and Devon, Molly (1998) *Screw the Roses, Send Me the Thorns: The Romance and Sexual Sorcery of Sadomasochism*, Connecticut: Mystic Rose Books.

Morton, James (1999) *Sex Crimes and Misdemeanours*, London: Little, Brown & Company (UK).

Muncie, John (1999) *Youth and Crime: A Critical Introduction*, London: Sage.

Newcombe, R. (1992) 'A Researcher Reports from the Rave', *Druglink*, Jan./Feb.

Norris, C. and Armstrong, G. (1999) *The Maximum Surveillance Society: The Rise of CCTV*, London: Berg

Nuttall, Jeff and Carmichael, Rodick (1977) *Common Factors/ Vulgar Factions*, London, Henley and Boston: Routledge & Kegan Paul.

Office for National Statistics (1999) *Recent Trends in Deaths from Homicide in England and Wales*, London: Office for National Statistics.

Orwell, George [1941] (1965) 'The Art of Donald McGill', reprinted in *Decline of the English Murder and Other Essays*, Harmondsworth: Penguin.

Parker, Howard, Aldridge, Judith and Measham, Fiona (1998)

Illegal Leisure: The Normalization of Adolescent Recreational Drug Use, London and New York: Routledge.

Parsons, Carl (1999) *Education, Exclusion and Citizenship*, London and New York: Routledge.

Pegg, Bob (1981) *Rites and Riots: Folk Customs of Britain and Europe*, Poole: Blandford Press.

Pettitt, T. (1984) 'Here Comes I Jack Straw: English Folk Drama and Social Revolt', *Folklore 95*: 1.

Pickford, J. (ed.) (2000) *Youth Criminal Justice Theory and Practice*, London: Cavendish.

Pratt, A. (1901) ' "Push" Larrikinism in Australia', *Blackwoods Magazine*, MXXIX, July.

Presdee, Mike (1988) *The Muck of Ages*, unpublished.

Presdee, Mike (1990) 'Deregulation, Youth Policies and the Creation of Crime', in Ian Taylor (ed.) *The Social Effects of Free Market Policies: An International Text*, London: Harvester Wheatsheaf, pp. 175–196.

Presdee, Mike (1993) 'Violence dans les villes', *Les Annales de la Recherche Urbaine* 54: 68–69.

Presdee, Mike (1994) 'Young People, Culture, and the Construction of Crime: Doing Wrong versus Doing Crime' in Gregg Barak, *Varieties of Criminology: Reading from a Dynamic Discipline*, London and Westport: Praeger.

Presdee, Mike (1999) 'Le Carnival et la mise en scène du crime: Les jeunes, les couteaux et autres armes' in *La Création sociale: sociétés, cultures, imaginaires*, Grenoble: Université Pierre Mendes France.

Quinney, Richard (1994) 'Crime as a Problem of Human Existence: Thinking about Erich Fromm'. Paper presented at the annual meeting of the American Society of Criminology, Miami, November 1994.

Redhead, Steve (ed.) (1993) *Rave Off: Politics and Deviance in Contemporary Youth Culture*, Aldershot: Avebury.

Redhead, Steve (1997) *Subcultures to Clubcultures: An Introduction to Popular Cultural Studies*, London: Blackwell.

Redhead, Steve (ed.) (1998) *The Clubcultures Reader: Readings in Popular Cultural Studies*, with Derek Wynne and Justin O'Connor, Oxford: Blackwell.

Reik, Theodore (1962) *Masochism in Sex and Society*, New York: Grove Press.

Reynolds, S. (1998) 'Living Dream or Living Death' in Steve

Redhead (ed.) *The Clubcultures Reader: Readings in Popular Cultural Studies*, Oxford: Blackwell.

Rojek, Chris (1995) *Decentring Leisure: Rethinking Leisure Theory*, London: Sage.

Rose, C. (1991) *Design after Dark: The Story of Dancefloor Style*, London: Thames & Hudson.

Rose, Nikolas (1989) *Governing the Soul: The Shaping of the Private Self*, London and New York: Routledge.

Ross, Andrew and Rose, Tricia (1994) *Microphone Fiends: Youth Music,Youth Culture*, London and New York: Routledge.

Rouget, G. (1990) *La Musique et la trance*, Paris: Galimard.

Runciman, W. G. (ed.) (1978) *Max Weber: Selections in Translation*, trans. Eric Mathews, Cambridge: Cambridge University Press.

Sartre, Jean-Paul (1957) *Being and Nothingness*, London: Methuen.

Sartre, Jean-Paul (1963) *Saint Genet: Actor and Martyr*, trans. Bernard Frechtman, New York.

Schechner, Richard (1988) *Performance Theory*, London and New York: Routledge.

Schechner, Richard (1993) *The Future of Ritual*, London and New York: Routledge.

Schneider, R. (1997) *The Explicit Body in Performance*, London and New York: Routledge.

Schopenhauer, A. [1818] (1969) *On the Basis of Morality*, Indianapolis: Bobbs-Merrill.

Shields, R. (1991) *Places on the Margins: Alternative Geographies of Modernity*, London: Routledge.

Simmel, G. (1903) 'Soziologie des Raumes', *Jahrbuch für Gesetzgebung, Verwaltung und Volkswirtschaft*, 27: 27–71.

Simmel, G. (1950) *The Sociology of Georg Simmel*, trans. Kurt H. Wolff, New York: The Free Press.

Simmel, G. (1990) *The Philosophy of Money*, London: Routledge.

Skvorecky, Josef (1980) 'Red Music' in *The Bass Saxophone*, London.

Slater, Don (1997) *Consumer Culture and Modernity*, Cambridge: Polity Press.

Social Exclusion Unit (1999) *Bridging the Gap*, London: HMSO.

Sontag, Susan (1977) *About Photography*, New York: Delta.

Sparks, Richard (1992) *Television and the Drama Of Crime: Moral Tales and the Place of Crime in Public Life*, Buckingham and Philadelphia: Open University Press.

Stallybrass, P. and White, A. (1986) *The Politics and Poetry of Transgression*, London: Methuen.

Stanley, Christopher (1996) *Urban Excess and the Law: Capital, Culture and Desire*, London: Cavendish.

Storey, John (1996) *Cultural Studies and the Study of Popular Culture: Theories and Methods*, Edinburgh: Edinburgh University Press.

Storey, John (1999) *Cultural Consumption and Everyday Life*, London/Sydney/Auckland: Arnold.

Sweetman, Paul (1997) 'Marked Bodies, Oppositional Identities? Tattooing, Piercing and the Ambiguity of Resistance'. Paper presented at the British Sociological Association Conference, York, 1997.

Tambling, Jeremy (1990) *Confession: Sexuality, Sin, the Subject*, Manchester and New York: Manchester University Press.

Taylor, Ian (ed.) (1990) *The Social Effects of Free Market Policies*, London and New York: Harvester Wheatsheaf.

Thompson, Bill (1994) *Sadomasochism: Painful Perversion or Pleasurable Play?*, London: Cassell.

Thornton, Sarah (1995) *Club Cultures: Music, Media and Subcultural Capital*, Cambridge: Polity Press.

Turner, V. (1979) *Process, Performance and Pilgrimage*, New Delhi: Concept.

Turner, V. (1983) 'Body, Brain and Culture', *Zygon* 18 (3): 221–245.

Turner, V. (1985) *On the Edge of the Bush*, Tucson: University of Arizona Press.

Veblen, Thorstein (1953) *The Theory of the Leisure Class: An Economic Study of Institutions*, New York: Mentor Books.

Weber, Max (1948) *The Protestant Ethic and the Spirit of Capitalism*, New York: Charles Scribner's Sons.

Weber, Max (1978) *Selections in Translation*, ed. W. G. Runciman, Cambridge: Cambridge University Press.

Websdale, Neil (1998) 'Police Homicide Files as Situated Media Substrates: An Exploratory Essay'. Paper presented at the American Society of Criminology conference, Chicago 1998.

Weeks, Jeffrey (1985) *Sexuality and Its Discontents*, London: Routledge.

Weschler, L. (1999) *Boggs: A Comedy of Values*, Chicago: University of Chicago Press.

White, R. (1990) *No Space of Their Own*, Cambridge: Cambridge University Press.

Williams, R. (1974) *Television, Technology and Cultural Forms*, London: Fontana.

Williams, R. S. (1982) *Dream Worlds: Mass Consumption in the Late 19th Century in France*, Berkeley: University of California Press.

Williamson, Judith (1988) *Consuming Passions: The Dynamic of Popular Culture*, London: Marion Boyars.

Willis, Paul (1978) *Profane Culture*, London: Routledge & Kegan Paul.

Willis, Paul (1990) *Common Culture*, Milton Keynes: Open University Press.

Index

(Italicized page numbers refer to plates.)